Praise for *Lab Class*

"*Lab Class* is easy both to read and follow. It is informative and sets up [illegible] open process built around collaborative trusting learning. It gives examples of the professional growth that can be gained by teachers, which in turn stimulates student learning and growth. The Lab Class will be a comprehensive approach to building depth and collective efficacy."

Trish Gooch, Education Officer of Primary Curriculum
Northern Territory Catholic Education Office
Northern Territory, Australia

"Lisa Cranston's book is a valuable resource for educators who want to replicate this model of Lab classrooms. The explanations, steps in the process, and templates and tools provided are described very well. The author describes a clear method for implementation of the Lab process. Anyone desiring to implement this process should use this book to guide them completely through the planning and implantation stages."

Chris Bryan, Senior Consultant
Learning Forward
Oxford, OH

"*Lab Class* is a great professional learning structure, one that can be adapted to different organizational models and that can be used for any content area. The power of this structure is definitely worth sharing, and Lisa Cranston obviously has experience and knowledge that is valuable. *Lab Class* will be a great tool for pushing learning walks to a deeper level of learning for educators."

Ellen S. Perconti, Superintendent
Mary M. Knight School District
Elma, WA

"The content of *Lab Class* is very relevant to the current need in the field, especially in light of the high impact that collective teacher efficacy has on [John] Hattie's list. The Lab Class process is a step forward in this direction, while offering capacity-building for the practitioners and learners. Whereas learning walks and instructional rounds may be a good beginning, they do often carry a sense of a 'top-down' experience directed by administrators or the district. The Lab Class is a more grass-roots effort in deepening practices. For districts that have implemented learning walks and instructional rounds for a while, the Lab Class is a comprehensive approach to building depth and collective efficacy."

Marine Avagyan, EdD, Director of Curriculum & Instruction
Saugus Union School District
Santa Clarita, CA

"This book is an invaluable tool for school leaders and education professionals looking to improve professional learning. The unique professional learning model described in the text must be embraced by education professionals. Much of today's professional development is 'sit and get' and is generally not an effective method of professional development. *Lab Class* is a crucial step in the right direction for improving professional development."

Miriam A. DeCock, Classroom Instructor
Wadena-Deer Creek Public Schools
Wadena, MN

Lab Class

Lab Class

Professional Learning Through Collaborative Inquiry and Student Observation

Lisa Cranston

FOR INFORMATION:

Corwin
A SAGE Company
2455 Teller Road
Thousand Oaks, California 91320
(800) 233-9936
www.corwin.com

SAGE Publications Ltd.
1 Oliver's Yard
55 City Road
London EC1Y 1SP
United Kingdom

SAGE Publications India Pvt. Ltd.
B 1/I 1 Mohan Cooperative Industrial Area
Mathura Road, New Delhi 110 044
India

SAGE Publications Asia-Pacific Pte. Ltd.
3 Church Street
#10-04 Samsung Hub
Singapore 049483

Acquisitions Editor: Dan Alpert
Associate Editor: Lucas Schleicher
Editorial Assistant: Mia Rodriguez
Production Editor: Jane Martinez
Copy Editor: Deanna Noga
Typesetter: C&M Digitals (P) Ltd.
Proofreader: Sally Jaskold
Indexer: Judy Hunt
Cover Designer: Michael Dubowe
Marketing Manager: Lisa Lysne

Printed in the United States of America

Library of Congress Cataloging-in-Publication Data

Names: Cranston, Lisa, author.

Title: Lab class : professional learning through collaborative inquiry and student observation / Lisa Cranston.

Description: Thousand Oaks, California : Corwin, 2019. | Includes bibliographical references and index.

Identifiers: LCCN 2018003611 | ISBN 9781544327952 (pbk. : alk. paper)

Subjects: LCSH: Professional learning communities. | Teachers—Professional relationships. | Observation (Educational method) | Teaching teams.

Classification: LCC LB1731 .C675 2019 | DDC 370.71/1—dc23
LC record available at https://lccn.loc.gov/2018003611

This book is printed on acid-free paper.

SFI label applies to text stock

18 19 20 21 22 10 9 8 7 6 5 4 3 2 1

CONTENTS

Visit the companion website at
resources.corwin.com/LabClass
for downloadable resources.

PREFACE

In our work supporting teachers and administrators in a large school district, my colleagues and I were searching for a way to provide personalized and precise professional learning that would support educators in helping their students reach their fullest potential.

Educators and administrators told us in exit tickets, feedback surveys, and conversations that they preferred school-based professional learning. They appreciated focusing on the goals set out in their school improvement plan, their students' needs, and their own professional learning interests instead of attending large sit-and-get style workshops. They also appreciated the opportunity to visit one another's classrooms. Based on this feedback, we hosted many after-school workshops at schools and built in time for classroom visits and tours. We wondered how to deepen the learning from these observations so that we could get beyond idea sharing and explore the beliefs and research behind the classroom practice.

During a presentation at a Learning Forward conference, Lucy West talked about shifting classroom observations from "viewing a master teacher" to "providing an opportunity for teachers to view one another's practice and talk about where they are in their learning journey. What are they still wondering? What are they trying to figure out?" At this same time, we were beginning to use collaborative teacher inquiry as a model for professional learning. Collaborative inquiry is a process that engages educators in examining the impact of their instructional actions on student learning (Donohoo, 2013). We wondered: ***What if we combined school-based collaborative inquiry with purposeful classroom observation of student learning?*** And thus, the Lab Class model was born. That first year, we used Lab Class with a group of teachers at one school, but we knew that the learning would be richer if teachers networked with teachers from other schools (Katz, Dack, & Earl, 2009). For the next few years, we created Lab Class networks—teachers were engaged in Lab Class at their school and networking with teachers from other schools who were also participating in Lab Class.

Then a new group of teachers approached us. They had heard about Lab Class and wanted to participate but no one in their school was interested in learning more about inquiry-based learning, which was the instructional strategy they wanted to explore. Could we support a group of teachers, each the only one at their school, interested in Lab Class? And so the model continued to evolve. Over the next few years, we continued to refine the Lab Class model, developing templates, agendas, and overviews to support other facilitators who wanted to use Lab Class with their schools. This book is the culmination of that work.

This book is intended to support facilitators who want to engage in powerful school-based learning with their teams using the Lab Class model. Facilitators can be those in formal or informal leadership roles—teacher-leaders, curriculum specialists, instructional coaches, building-level administrators, district administrators, and others. In this book, facilitators will find

- an explicit, scaffolded approach that specifically outlines practical steps to professional development using Lab Class;
- a clear breakdown of all the components of the model in reader-friendly language;
- extensive organizational structures, readable tables, and proposed agendas for full-day, half-day, and Professional Learning Community timeframes;
- references to research to support the principles of Lab Class; and
- multiple examples and vignettes from a range of grade and subject areas.

Adults are motivated to learn when organizational structures allow them to work together and learn from one another on a continuous basis (Datnow, 2011; Groundwater-Smith & Mockler, 2009; Riveros, Newton, & Burgess, 2012). As we move from a model of professional development as an event where teachers passively receive information toward professional learning as a reflective process where teachers are collaboratively building knowledge, there is a need for resources to support collaborative school-based learning. Without organizational support and intentional facilitation, school-based learning does not transform teacher practice (Katz, 2010; Riveros et al., 2012). This book clearly describes how the Lab Class model of school-based learning enhances the classroom experience and learning for students as well as the professional learning of facilitators and educators.

I have had the privilege of working with many educators throughout my career who have influenced my thinking and supported my learning. Thank you to my colleagues who pushed my thinking forward and who were always ready to engage in deep and meaningful conversations about our work. Thank you to the many educators and administrators who allowed me to engage as a co-learner with them in Lab Class. Your enthusiasm for your own professional learning as well as your passion for your students' learning inspires me.

Thank you to all the consultants, coaches, Student Work Study teachers and other central office team members whose vision helped to shape Lab Class as it grew and evolved. I'm grateful to have had the opportunity to work with and learn from you.

Dr. Clara Howitt, thank you for believing in our vision and providing us with the resources to bring this vision to reality.

Thank you to Dan Alpert at Corwin and to Jenni Donohoo for their ongoing support during this publishing process and to everyone at Corwin who helped bring this book to fruition.

And none of this would be possible without the love and support of my husband, John, and my daughters, Shelby and Madison. Thank you for your encouragement and your patience. You are my world!

Publisher's Acknowledgments

Corwin gratefully acknowledges the contributions of the following reviewers:

Jessica Antosz
Manager of Professional Learning and Development
British Columbia Principals' and Vice-Principals Association
Vancouver, British Columbia, Canada

Marine Avagyna
Director of Curriculum & Instruction
Saugus Union School District
Santa Clarita, California

Chris Bryan
Senior Consultant
Learning Forward
Oxford, Ohio

Claudia A. Danna
Adjunct Professor and Educational Consultant
Sacred Heart University, Griswold Campus
Griswold, Connecticut

Miriam A. DeCock
Classroom Instructor
Wadena-Deer Creek ISD 2155
Wadena, Minnesota

Patricia Gooch
Education Officer, Primary Curriculum
Northern Territory Catholic Education Office
Berrimah, Northern Territory, Australia

J. Blanca O. López
Employee Quality Coordinator
Ysleta ISD
El Paso, Texas

Ellen S. Perconti
Superintendent
Mary M. Knight School District
Elma, Washington

Lucy West
Coach/Consultant
Metamorphosis Teaching Learning Communities
New York City, New York

ABOUT THE AUTHOR

Lisa Cranston has over 30 years of experience as an educator and has taught kindergarten to Grade 4. She has also worked as an instructional coach for literacy and mathematics, as an educational consultant for kindergarten and primary grades, and provided induction for new teachers and their mentors. In her role as a curriculum consultant, Lisa and her colleagues developed the Lab Class model to support professional learning for teachers and administrators. This model reflects Lisa's beliefs that collaboration is key to professional learning and that educational leaders must engage as co-learners with teachers if they are to create sustainable change in practice.

Lisa recently completed a doctoral degree in educational leadership at Western University and has a master's degree in curriculum studies from the University of Windsor and an undergraduate degree in early childhood education from Ryerson University in Toronto. She is a consulting editor for the National Association for Young Children's journal *Teaching Young Children* and a presenter for The MEHRIT Centre. She enjoys traveling with her two daughters and her husband or relaxing in their home on the shores of Lake Erie near the vineyards of Southern Ontario.

An Overview of Lab Class

> The idea is that significant *changes in student learning, engagement and success* depend on deep and sustained *changes in the practices in classrooms and schools*, and that these changes will emerge from the *teacher learning (professional knowledge creation and sharing)* that occurs through interaction within and across schools in networks.
>
> —Katz, Dack, & Earl (2009)

What Is Lab Class?

Lab Class is a professional learning structure combining the "teacher as researcher" approach of collaborative inquiry (Donohoo, 2013) with descriptive observation and analysis of student learning in the classroom. In Lab Class teachers examine the impact of instructional practice on student learning through collaborative planning, teaching, assessment, and observation and consider how evidence-informed instructional approaches can be implemented in their classrooms. Time for professional learning is embedded in Lab Class and is in response to observations of student learning; teachers learn from their students as well as from one another and with one another. It is a structure that can be effectively used by teachers from kindergarten to Grade 12.

As mentioned in the preface, the Lab Class structure grew out of our work as coaches and consultants using collaborative inquiry as a professional learning model with educators. Collaborative inquiry is a four-stage model where teachers are: Framing the Problem; Collecting Evidence; Analyzing Evidence; and Documenting, Sharing, and Celebrating (Donohoo, 2013). Educators and administrators used collaborative inquiry to focus on the goals set out in their school improvement plan, their students' needs, and their own professional learning interests. But educators told us they wanted to see inquiry in action and get into one another's classrooms. As a result, the

Lab Class model was created to combine the elements of collaborative inquiry with purposeful classroom observation and analysis of student learning. The examples and quotations in this book are from students, teachers, and administrators who participated in Lab Class projects over the past 7 years in our school district. (The names of people and places have been changed to ensure anonymity.)

While Lab Class is similar to other professional learning models such as *Instructional Rounds* (City, Elmore, Fiarman, & Teitel, 2011) and *Lesson Study* (Stepanek, Appel, Leong, Turner Mangan, & Mitchell, 2007) in that it is school-based, it has many unique features that set it apart. In Lab Class, teachers observe student learning from an asset stance, concentrating on students' learning strengths rather than their deficits. Observations are focused on three or four carefully selected marker students or "students of mystery"—these are students who are able to achieve but are not achieving, with no clear reason for their lack of progress (Ontario Ministry of Education, 2012). During Lab Class, teachers engage in professional learning using research and professional resources to determine next steps. The time frame for Lab Class can range from a few months up to a school year, and the number of participants can range from as few as three teachers to large groups of 20 teachers. Each of these features is explored in greater depth in subsequent chapters.

Lab Class can be used by several teachers at one school or by a network of teachers across multiple schools. The concept of networks is wide-ranging in professional learning models; in Lab Class, we refer to networks as groups of teachers within one school or across several schools who are engaging in collaborative professional learning to improve their teaching and ultimately improve student achievement. Capacity building in schools is strengthened by groups of teachers coming together to share and analyze their work, but school-to-school learning networks give schools and teachers an even wider range of ideas and choices and move good teaching around the system (Stoll, 2009).

	LAB CLASS	INSTRUCTIONAL ROUNDS (CITY ET AL., 2011)	LESSON STUDY (STEPANEK ET AL., 2007)
Definition	Lab Class is a professional learning structure combining teacher collaborative inquiry with descriptive observation and analysis of student learning in the classroom.	"Rounds is a four-step process: identifying a problem of practice, observing, debriefing, and focusing on the next level of work" (p. 6).	"Lesson study is a professional development practice in which teachers collaborate to develop a lesson plan, teach and observe the lesson to collect data on student learning, and use their observations to refine their lesson" (p. 2).
Participants	Teachers, Coaches/ Consultants Administrators	Superintendents Administrators Coaches/Consultants Teachers	Teachers

	LAB CLASS	INSTRUCTIONAL ROUNDS (CITY ET AL., 2011)	LESSON STUDY (STEPANEK ET AL., 2007)
Who is observed?	Marker students of teachers who are participating in Lab Class	Teachers and students in three to four classrooms at the schools of the instructional rounds network participants. The observed teachers may not necessarily be part of the instructional rounds network (p. 6).	Teachers and students in the classrooms of teachers who are participating in lesson study
Development of an Inquiry Question	Yes	No	No
Development of Theories of Action	Yes	Yes	No
Embedded time for professional reading	Yes	No	No
School-based	Yes	Yes	Yes
How is learning shared?	Multiple and varied means—determined by the group	Recommendations from the network meeting for "next level of work" Scaling up the work over time (p. 183)	Research reports
Time frame	Four months to one school year	One day/month (p. 66)	Several school years

Table 1.1 Comparison of Professional Learning Models

The Lab Class Model—Step by Step

This resource is intended to act as a support for educators and facilitators interested in supporting colleagues in using the Lab Class process to engage in sustained professional learning. Lab Class takes place over a period of several months and begins with a Launch Meeting for all participants, including the school administrator. This is followed by several days of classroom observations, analysis, and professional learning spread over weeks or months, and Lab Class concludes with a final Consolidation Meeting. The steps of Lab Class, listed and outlined briefly below, are more fully explained in subsequent chapters. Templates and other resources for facilitators of Lab Class can be found in the Appendix.

A Visual Overview of Lab Class

Launch Meeting

- Overview and expectations
- Create norms
- Determine focus
- Develop inquiry question and theories of action
- Learn to be descriptive
- Walkthrough of Lab Class
- Select marker students
- Schedule observation visits

Classroom Observation Meetings

Review Norms, Inquiry Question, and Theories of Action

Overview from Host Teachers

Classroom Observations

Analysis of Observations

Next Steps and Professional Learning

Consolidation Meeting

- Review inquiry question and theories of action
- Summarize key learning for students and teachers
- Develop communication plan
- Next steps and professional learning

Preparing for Lab Class: Launch Meeting

1. *Determine a focus.* Teams develop their collaborative inquiry questions based on evidence about students' capabilities and areas for growth as well as their own professional curiosities using the frame: What is the impact of *this teacher practice* on *this student learning*?

2. *Learn to be descriptive.* City et al. (2011) noted that trying to simply observe what we see at the most basic descriptive level without inference or judgment is very difficult. Prior to engaging in the first classroom observation, teachers use photos and video clips of students engaged in learning to practice taking descriptive observations and provide feedback to each other on their progress.

3. *Discuss norms.* Each lab class group creates their own set of norms for the in-school classroom observations, which are reviewed before each classroom observation visit. Determine a schedule for classroom observation visits.

Engaging in Lab Class

On a subsequent day, the teachers engage in the first round of Lab Class observation visits. The number of additional rounds of observation visits will be determined by the budget for teacher release time and by the number of teachers participating in Lab Class. Every teacher participating in Lab Class, including the teachers being observed, is provided with supply coverage by an occasional teacher for each session.

4. *Take descriptive observations.* Participants visit classrooms to take descriptive observations of student conversations, actions, and products. Before heading to the classrooms, teachers meet briefly to review the norms and the team's inquiry question.

5. *Engage in individual analysis of observations.* Following the classroom observations each participant selects three to five observations that were descriptive, student-focused, asset-based, and related to the identified student learning focus to use for the analysis exercise.

6. *Cluster observations and name emerging trends.* With a curriculum consultant, coach, or teacher acting as facilitator, teachers work together to name and cluster emerging trends while they share the observations they had recorded.

7. *Identify conditions present.* Next, teachers discuss what conditions were present that allowed these trends to emerge. Conditions might include the routines and procedures in place, the organization of materials in the classroom environment, or specific teaching strategies.

8. *Determine next steps.* Based on the observations from Lab Class as well as the contributions from teachers whose classrooms were not observed, teachers collaboratively determine next steps and identify the resources that support the professional learning they need to engage in related to these next steps. These resources may include professional books, articles, district or government publications, curriculum materials, or human resources including support staff such as curriculum consultants, specialists, instructional coaches, or community partners.

9. *Document the learning of teachers and students.* Though many teachers are comfortable with documenting student learning, some struggle to document their own professional learning and growth. By providing time during Lab Class, teachers are supported in exploring a range of strategies for reflecting on and recording their own learning. Facilitators should review school and district policies on recording and sharing student learning prior to beginning Lab Class.

This cycle of Steps 4 through 9 is repeated on subsequent days until each teacher has had an opportunity to host observers in his or her classroom at least once.

Consolidation and Culmination of Lab Class

10. *Share the learning.* At the final networked learning session, teachers and administrators reflect on their own professional and personal learning, the students' learning, and their team's learning journey and consider with whom they want to share their learning and how they might share it.

Rationale for Lab Class

Years ago, professional development often took place at the district office or another central location such as a catering hall. Curriculum consultants from the central office were expected to have expertise in specific areas and to share their expertise with teachers, administrators, and the public. Teachers and administrators would leave their schools, attend a workshop, then return to their schools and be expected to implement whatever strategies had been introduced at the session. But researchers such as Borman (cited in Fullan, Hill, & Crévola, 2006) found little connection between professional development and changes in classroom instruction, even though the professional development was based on extensive modeling of specific instructional practices. Timperley and Alton-Lee (2008) noted that these highly prescriptive models of professional learning had little impact on student achievement whereas models of teacher inquiry had a more profound impact on teacher practice and knowledge.

There has been a dramatic shift in professional learning for educators and administrators and while there is still a time and a place for centralized workshops, much of the professional learning today takes place at the school through teacher inquiry. This inquiry learning is embedded in teachers' daily work and is directed by the needs of educators and students. Inquiry has the potential to create deep and significant changes in education, but there is neither a specific prescribed protocol for inquiry nor only one model that all educators should use (Ontario Ministry of Education, 2014). Lab Class is one model for professional learning that can be used by teachers to engage in teacher inquiry.

Goals of Lab Class

Regardless of the number of schools or the number of teachers participating, the overall goals of Lab Class remain the same—deprivatization of teacher practice, implementation of evidence-informed instructional approaches, development of teacher efficacy, the adoption of a learning-as-inquiry stance, creation of a culture of collaboration, and improved student achievement. While the goals are listed separately here, in practice they are intertwined and recursive.

Deprivatization of Teacher Practice

Teachers often work in isolation behind closed classroom doors and as a result, some

> teachers have come to regard autonomy and creativity—not rigorous, shared knowledge—as the badge of professionalism. . . . Teacher autonomy and isolation produce highly personalized forms of instruction and huge variations in teacher quality and effectiveness. In effect, each teacher is left to invent his or her own knowledge base—unexamined, untested, idiosyncratic, and potentially at odds with the knowledge from which other teachers may be operating. (Burney, 2004)

Each teacher who participates in Lab Class is able to observe in other teachers' classrooms while students are actively engaged in learning, and they also host at least one observation visit. Instead of attending off-school professional development workshops and returning to teach in solitude, professional learning has moved to the school and the classroom, and teachers are encouraged to share their work and their students' work. Changing the deeply rooted norm of privacy can be difficult as such a change requires risk-taking by teachers and leaders (Fullan, 2007).

By using a collaborative inquiry model to determine a specific area of inquiry, and through repeated observation and analysis of student learning with time for professional reflection and learning, Lab Class allows participants to move beyond superficial classroom observation to a more rigorous investigation of teacher practice, student learning, and the conditions that make learning possible. Deprivatization of teacher practice—through observation, analysis, collaboration, and sharing—can lead to teachers building new knowledge and problem solving together. Teachers have reported that Lab Class created an environment where they felt safe to take risks, learn, make mistakes, receive feedback, and refine their teaching practice. Through conversations about shared professional learning and observations of student learning, teachers create networks with colleagues within their own school and between schools. Teachers with differing teaching assignments discover commonalities and connections that last long after the formal Lab Class period has ended.

Implementation of Evidence-Informed Instructional Approaches

To be effective, Katz (2008) reminds us that learning communities must move beyond "story sharing" and into the area of cognitive dissonance and discomfort. While it is important to give teachers time to share stories from their classroom, we must move deeper in our examination of student learning to maximize the impact of Lab Class for teachers and for students. Time is provided for teachers during each Lab Class session to dig into professional reading and resources in response to their observations and analysis of student learning before determining their next steps for instruction. This is done to intentionally interrupt the tendency to observe student learning and then immediately jump to determining next steps for the student and for the instructor. Instead, based on their analysis of the classroom observations, teachers delve into research articles, curriculum documents, books, and other materials and seek input from resource staff to develop a much richer, research-based repertoire of strategies before determining the next step.

As teachers begin to implement new strategies, they are trying to master the skills required and their initial implementation may be disjointed and superficial (Hord & Hall, 2006). Lab Class provides a supportive environment in which teachers can apply new strategies over time in collaboration with peers at their own school and possibly at other schools. The balance of theory as well as practical classroom application strategies in a supportive environment increases the opportunities for teachers to experience some degree of success early in the process.

Students deserve educators in their schools who believe in themselves as well as each other and who are committed to facilitating student success and their own learning every school day. (Planche, 2009)

Development of Teacher Efficacy

Bandura (1994) defines *self-efficacy* as "people's judgments of their capabilities to organize and execute courses of action required to attain designated types of performances." In other words, if we have self-efficacy we believe that we have the knowledge and skills to perform a task and we believe that we can successfully perform the task in both typical and challenging conditions. A person with the same knowledge and skills may perform poorly, adequately, or extraordinarily depending on their self-efficacy (Bandura, 1993). It is a *belief* about one's ability, not actual ability (Leithwood, Mascall, & Jantzi, 2012).

Self-efficacy beliefs impact teacher motivation in several ways: They help determine what goals teachers set, how much effort they put in to achieving the goals, how long they persevere in their attempts, and their ability to deal with obstacles and setbacks (Bandura, 1993). The most effective way to create a strong sense of self-efficacy, for teachers and for students, is through mastery experiences. Lab Class provides a supportive environment for teachers to strive toward a collectively determined goal over a sustained period. Setbacks and challenges are shared with colleagues, and teachers can work together during the provided release time to discuss potential strategies and solutions. Because teachers in participating in Lab Class adjust their instructional practices over time, with the support of the other participants from their network and their administrators, they are more likely to achieve mastery and increase their own self-efficacy.

Teacher efficacy has been shown to have an impact on student efficacy (Bandura, 1993), and students with strong efficacy take academic risks and put forth greater effort. They display greater resilience, recovering more quickly from failures and ultimately finding more academic success.

Adoption of a Learning-as-Inquiry Stance

Inquiry involves wonder, curiosity, questioning, conversation, and cycles of reflection and action. Inquiry starts with defining a problem and then restating it so that it is a specific, personally relevant question. Teachers use a range of resources to learn more, plan how to enact their new learning, monitor their progress and their students' progress, and engage in discussion with colleagues throughout the process. As inquiry unfolds over time, teachers can consider and reconsider their thinking about pedagogy, student learning, the curriculum, and their connections with colleagues and the community. Inquiry involves action-oriented, reflective, and iterative interactions between self, context, and social domains (Schnellert & Butler, 2014).

This view of inquiry fits with our understanding of teaching and learning as multilayered and multifaceted, with connections between content areas as well as between all the learners, adult and children, in the classroom. Through discussions in Lab Class, as well as classroom observation experience and professional readings, teachers begin to reconsider the role of the teacher and the role of the student.

Each one of us needs to be able to play with the things that are coming out of the world of children. Each one of use needs to have curiosity, and we need to be able to try something new based on the ideas that we collect from the children as they go along. Life has to be somewhat agitated and upset, a bit restless, somewhat unknown. As life flows with the thoughts of the children, we need to be open, we need to change our ideas; we need to be comfortable with the restless nature of life. All of this changes the role of the teacher, a role that becomes much more difficult and complex. It also makes the world of the teacher more beautiful, something to become involved in. (Malaguzzi, 1994)

High impact professional learning models require teachers to move beyond using assessment and observations to inform their teaching; it requires them to use inquiry to investigate the impact of their teaching strategies on student learning and achievement (Timperley & Alton-Lee, 2008). As teachers monitor the impact of their practice on students, through observation and assessment, they adjust their goals and their teaching as required. Inquiry positions the teacher as co-learner and researcher—a much richer but more challenging role than that of teacher as implementer of prescribed programs.

Creating a Culture of Collaboration

As we deepen and extend school-based learning through Lab Class, facilitators must consider how to support teachers and administrators in creating and sustaining a culture of collaboration in their schools. *Culture* is defined as "the way we do things around here," and school culture is widely recognized as a key influence on the success of professional learning initiatives in schools (Cawsey, Deszca, & Ingols, 2016; Fullan, 2001; Schein, 2010).

Hart (1994) studied two middle schools in the same district that were both implementing a teacher development program with peer coaching and shared decision making. One school had a negative outcome. At this school, individualism and isolation were the prevailing norms. The principal was not visible, teachers were left on their own to succeed or fail, and there was no regular communication between the principal and the teachers. At the school with the more positive outcomes, the principal and teachers involved in the project worked closely together, and communicated regularly with the rest of the staff. There were frequent, ongoing opportunities for teachers to share feedback, and the learning was clearly connected to the core values of the school.

In an analysis of research on teacher leadership, York-Barr and Duke (2004) observed that "promoting instructional improvement requires an organizational culture that supports collaboration and continuous learning *and* that recognizes teachers as primary creators and re-creators of school culture" (p. 260; emphasis in original). They have organized the conditions that influence teacher leadership and collaboration into three categories:

1. *School culture and context*—Schools with a strong focus on learning and inquiry, encouragement for taking initiative and an expectation for teamwork, shared responsibility, and an expectation of professionalism were schools in which teacher leadership could flourish.
2. *Roles and relationships*—Important factors in this area included high degrees of trust amongst peers and with administrators, colleagues recognizing and supporting one another, and teachers given leadership opportunities that are aligned to the learning process as opposed to administrative or management tasks.
3. *Structures*—School-based, participatory structures that support learning and leading and are embedded in teachers' daily work.

Lab Class can provide the school-based, participatory structure to embed professional learning in teachers' practice. The challenge for participants and facilitators is to build on existing relationships and cultures at each school to foster an atmosphere of collegiality, shared responsibility, and trust.

Improved Student Achievement

Ultimately the goal of all that we do in education is student learning and achievement. In the Lab Class model, students have a voice. Teachers observe students and engage in conversations with them to deepen their own understanding of students' learning, and as a result, students learn that they have an audience for their ideas about their learning. Even our youngest students are capable of reflecting and articulating which strategies support them in their learning, and at times, they surprise us with the depth of their understanding.

Fullan and Hargreaves (2016) state that the quality of teaching is the most important in-school factor that affects student learning and achievement and the way to improve the quality of teaching is through professional learning and development. However, not all professional learning and development leads to improved quality of teaching and improved student learning. Supovitz (2006, cited in Katz, 2010) found that instead of "rigorous inquiry into challenges of instructional practice" professional learning communities engaged in work that was too diffused and unfocused to have any meaningful impact on teaching practice or student achievement.

Effective teacher professional learning, which leads to improved teacher practice and improved student achievement, must focus on pedagogy, provide opportunities for active, inquiry-based learning, allow for collective participation in learning, be sustainable over time, and take place in a supportive organizational culture (van Veen, Zwart, & Meirink, 2012). The principles of Lab Class align with these indicators of effective professional learning and suggest that using this model will lead to powerful professional learning, which in turn will impact student achievement.

Considerations for Launching Lab Class

Before beginning the Lab Class model, there are several considerations for facilitators, administrators, and potential participants to ponder.

Consideration 1: Voluntary Participation

In our experience, voluntary participation rather than forced participation has led to greater engagement, deeper professional learning, and more profound impact on teaching practice. Lab Class is conducted over a long period of time, often several months, and participants are expected to attend multiple full-day or half-day sessions. This requires a degree of commitment that is unlikely to be found when teachers are forced to participate. On many occasions, we noticed that teachers who chose not to participate in Lab Class became curious about the learning their colleagues were engaging in, and the nonparticipants asked questions, borrowed resources, and became interested in participating in other forms of professional learning. The Lab Class participants acted as mentors and coaches for their nonparticipant colleagues.

Consideration 2: Clear Expectations

While it is not necessary to have the full schedule of Lab Class observation visits determined prior to the Launch Meeting, it is important to ensure that everyone understand the expectations of participants in Lab Class:

- Host at least one observation visit
- Attend all sessions over a period of 3 months to 10 months (except in cases of emergency or illness)
- Participate actively in professional learning; these are not "sit and get" workshops
- Share their learning, formally or informally, with others in the school, in the Lab Class Network, or in the district

Consideration 3: School-Based Learning

It is nonnegotiable that the classroom observations must take place at the participating schools. When the Lab Class model involves a network between two or more schools, it is important that the participating schools each host at least one networked meeting of all participants. This may involve some planning ahead to find a place for the group to meet, and teachers may have to carpool if parking space is limited, but the benefits far outweigh any inconveniences.

Consideration 4: Administrator Involvement

In an analysis of research done over 20 years, York-Barr and Duke (2004) found that the relationship between the principal and teacher leaders was a strong influence on teacher leadership. Especially important were open lines of communication and ongoing feedback. Smylie and Hart (2000) note

> the research is clear that principals play a vital role in the development and maintenance of social capital among teachers. Their contributions come through creating structures and occasions for interaction to take place and for social bonds to form, mobilizing groups for interaction, and establishing broad support systems. Beyond these managerial functions, principals play an active role in fostering productive social relations within the structures they may help create. (p. 436)

Time after time participants in Lab Class have said that administrator support is key. With administrator support, teachers feel safe trying new approaches to teaching, knowing that their principal understands that there may be a learning curve while teachers implement new practices designed to support student learning. Ideally, administrators should attend all the meetings and engage as co-learners with the teachers.

Consideration 5: Teacher Release Time

Teachers need occasional teacher or supply teacher coverage to participate in Lab Class. To provide that coverage, facilitators and teachers may need to consider what model will work best for their situation. If it is not possible to provide full-day coverage for the Launch Meeting and half-day coverage for the observation days, then educators may want to consider using time allotted for professional learning communities for Lab Class. Professional learning communities (PLCs) consist of teachers engaging together in challenges of practice. Through investigations and exploration of possible solutions, teaching practice grows more sophisticated and powerful because teachers construct knowledge and develop common understandings (Supovitz, cited in Katz, 2010). While PLCs are often present in district language, poor understanding of the concept leads to problems with enactment. Without organizational support and intentional facilitation, PLCs do not transform teacher practice (Katz, 2010; Riveros, Newton, & Burgess, 2012). Lab Class is one possible model for providing structure and intentional facilitation to PLCs, which may in turn increase the possibility of effecting change on teacher practice.

Consideration 6: The Role of the Facilitator

While Lab Class provides the structure to guide teachers through the learning process, a facilitator is needed to support the group in moving through the steps, to gather professional learning resources, to ensure all voices are heard, to ensure the discussions are asset-based, and to keep student achievement and learning at the forefront of the work. Lab Class can be facilitated by educational consultants, coaches, or other teacher leaders from the school or the district. Facilitators may find the use of the templates provided in this book helpful for guiding teachers in the Lab Class process. Troubleshooting tips are provided at the end of each chapter with strategies for addressing challenges that may arise during the different steps of Lab Class.

Organizational Models of Lab Class

There are three models of Lab Class: Multiple Teachers/One School, Multiple Teachers/Multiple Schools, and One Teacher/Multiple Schools. In Multiple Teachers/One School (see Figure 1.1) several teachers located at one school engage in Lab Class together. This model allows for flexible scheduling and can often build on preexisting relationships among the teachers. In the Multiple Teachers/Multiple Schools (see Figure 1.2) there are two or more schools with two or more teachers at each school participating in Lab Class. Last, in Single

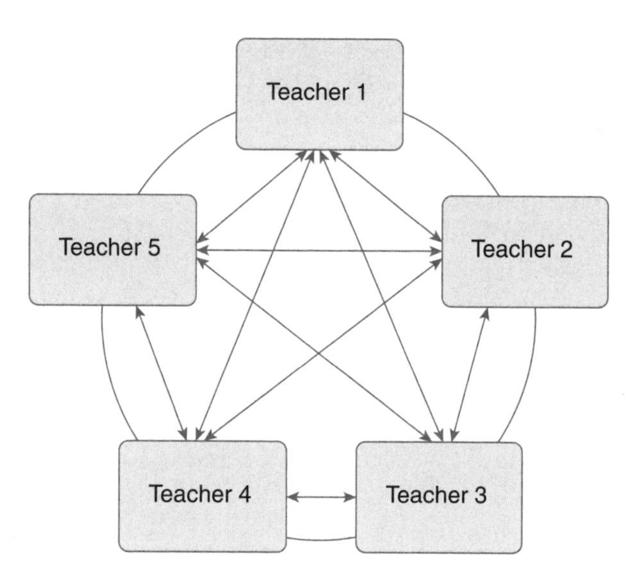

Figure 1.1 Multiple Teachers/One School

Teachers/Multiple Schools (see Figure 1.3) there are two or more schools with only one teacher at each school participating in Lab Class. Examples of each of the three models are provided in Chapter 5.

Multiple Teachers/One School

In this model of lab class, three to six teachers at one school conduct Lab Class to investigate an area of common interest. The teachers may be from a range of grade levels or from similar grade levels. More than six teachers in a Lab Class group can make scheduling classroom observation visits challenging. If there are more than six teachers interested in participating in Lab Class at one school, organizers should consider creating two or more smaller Lab Class groups, each with three to six teachers per school.

Example: Multiple Teachers/One School

Several primary teachers at an urban school were concerned about a perceived oral language vocabulary deficit in their students. With the support of their principal and vice-principal and the primary curriculum consultant from central office, they engaged in Lab Class for 6 months using the inquiry question: "What is the impact of engaging in dramatic play on the development of students' expressive oral language?"

Lab class participants: Three kindergarten teachers, two Grade 1 teachers, one Grade 2 teacher, principal, vice-principal, and a curriculum consultant took part in Lab Class at this school. The speech-language pathologist who was assigned to the school and visited the staff once every 2 weeks was also invited to support this project. Since her schedule did not always coincide with the date of the meetings, she would check in with the administrators and teachers during each visit to offer support, answer questions, and suggest possible resources for students and for teacher professional learning.

Schedule: Teachers were provided release time for the Launch Meeting for a full day, and then subsequent release time of half a day for each observation session. All meetings were conducted at the school, which made it much easier for the administrators to participate in Lab Class. Since the kindergarten teachers were very comfortable with using drama to support student learning, the initial classroom visits were in the kindergarten classroom. By the time the Grade 1 and Grade 2 teachers were hosting observation visits, they had begun to use drama in a variety of ways to support student oral language development.

The schedule was flexible, and teachers could choose to have the observation sessions closer together to condense the schedule, or it could be extended to allow for repeat observation visits if time and budget allowed. In this example, the budget allowed for only one visit to each classroom.

MEETING	PURPOSE	DATE
Launch Meeting	Determine inquiry question Establish schedule of observation visits	October Full Day
Lab Class Observation Session	Observation: Kindergarten Classrooms A & B	Late November Half Day
Lab Class Observation Session	Observation: Kindergarten Classroom C & Grade 1 Classroom D	Mid-January Half Day
Lab Class Observation Session	Observation: Grade 1 Classroom E & Grade 2 Classroom F	Late February Half Day
Final Meeting	Consolidation and Planning for Sharing	Early April Full Day

Table 1.2 Overview of Lab Class—Potential Overall Schedule for Multiple Teachers/One School

Available for download at **resources.corwin.com/LabClass**

Multiple Teachers/Multiple Schools

The Multiple Teachers/Multiple Schools model is similar to the previous model in that multiple teachers at a school, with similar or different teaching assignments, are investigating a topic of interest. However, in this model the teachers at one school are networked with teachers at another school or schools who are also interested in investigating the same topic. Depending on the number of teachers at each school, a network may consist of two to four schools. If there are more than four schools interested in participating in a Networked Lab Class, organizers should consider creating several smaller networks with two to four schools in each network.

Example: Multiple Teachers/Multiple Schools

Teachers at three different schools in one district whose assignments included kindergarten, Grades 1 through 4, as well as a teacher of a self-contained special

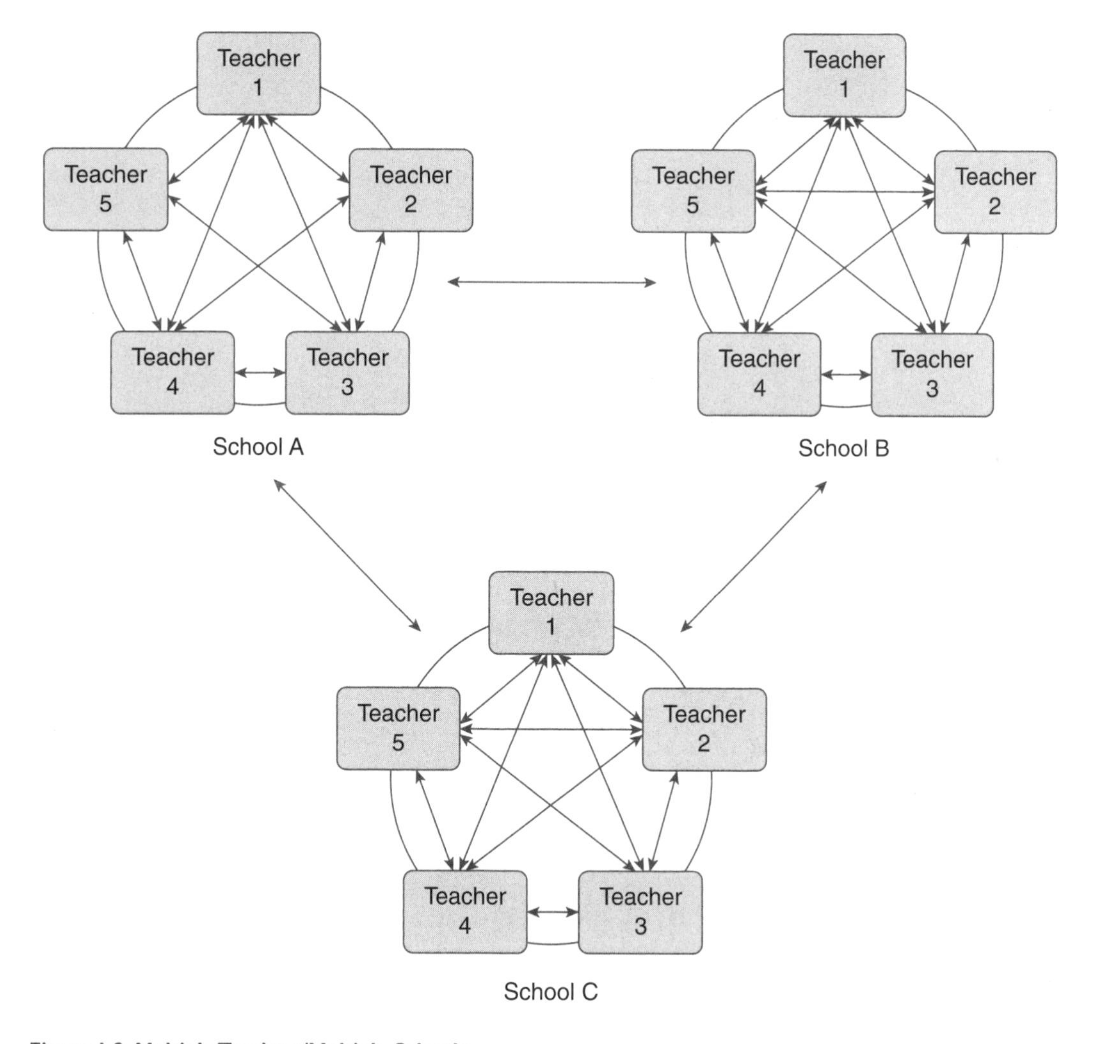

Figure 1.2 Multiple Teachers/Multiple Schools

education class for students with special academic needs were interested in exploring the impact of inquiry learning on student achievement. Each school group determined their own inquiry question based on their students and the teachers' own professional curiosities.

- *First Street School:* What is the impact of intentionally creating an inquiry learning environment that provokes student action, dialogue, and reflection on students' expression of their learning?
- *Second Street School:* What is the impact of explicitly teaching oral language on students' confidence and ability to express their thoughts, questions, and ideas within an inquiry-based environment?
- *Third Street School:* What is the impact of responsive educator actions on students' ability to demonstrate their critical thinking?

Schedule: Teachers were provided release time for the Launch Meeting for a full day, and then subsequent release time of half a day for each observation session. All meetings were held at schools including the Networked Lab Class Meetings. We began the multiple teacher/multiple school Lab Class with a Launch Meeting for teachers and administrators from all schools at one central location. With multiple schools, our meetings alternated between Networked Lab Class Meetings, which included teachers and administrators (when possible) from all three schools, and Classroom Observation Lab Classes, which occurred at each individual school and were attended only by the teachers at that school. Classroom Observation Lab Classes occurred between the Networked Lab Class Meetings, and each school selected a date and time (morning or afternoon) for their Classroom Observation Lab Class that was most convenient for their staff and schedule.

MEETING	PURPOSE	DATE
Networked Lab Class Meeting—all schools attend	• Determine inquiry question • Establish schedule of observation visits	Late October Full Day
Lab Class Observation—held separately at each individual school	Each school chooses a half-day that works best for their schedule to observe in two teachers' classrooms. This visit must take place before the next Networked Lab Class Meeting.	Late October to Mid-December Half Day

MEETING	PURPOSE	DATE
Networked Lab Class Meeting—all schools attend at First Street School	• Share student learning and professional learning with grade-level colleagues • Classroom observation visits • Engage in exploration of professional resources • Determine next steps	Mid-December Full Day
Lab Class Observation—held separately at each individual school	Each school chooses a half-day that works best for their schedule to observe in two teachers' classrooms. This visit must take place before the next Networked Lab Class Meeting.	Mid-December to Late January Half Day
Networked Lab Class Meeting—all schools attend at Second Street School	• Share student learning and professional learning with grade-level colleagues • Classroom observation visits • Engage in exploration of professional resources • Determine next steps	Early February Full Day
Lab Class Observation—held separately at each individual school	Each school chooses a half-day that works best for their schedule to observe in two teachers' classrooms. This visit must take place before the next Networked Lab Class Meeting.	Early February to Late March Half Day
Final Networked Lab Class Meeting—all schools attend at Third Street School	• Share student learning and professional learning with grade-level colleagues • Classroom observation visits • Determine strategies for sharing our learning • Consolidation	Early April Full Day

Table 1.3 Overview of Lab Class—Potential Overall Schedule for Multiple Teachers/Multiple Schools

online resources Available for download at **resources.corwin.com/LabClass**

One Teacher/Multiple Schools

This model is useful when there are isolated teachers who are interested in exploring a topic but there are no colleagues at their school who are able or willing to participate in Lab Class. It is also a suitable model when participating teachers have unique teaching assignments and are looking to network with colleagues at other schools with the same assignment.

Example: One Teacher/Multiple Schools

A school district designated one teacher as the music teacher in each elementary school; depending on school enrollment this could be a full-time or part-time assignment. Music teachers from eight schools used Lab Class to investigate their inquiry question: What is the impact of inquiry-based learning on student perseverance in instrumental music class? The music teachers often found that items on the staff meeting agenda had little relevance for them and their teaching assignment, and the questions that were pertinent to their assignment were not applicable to their colleagues. Lab Class became an informal support network where they could discuss questions and concerns pertinent to their assignment that were not necessarily relevant for their colleagues with homeroom assignments.

Schedule: Because some teachers were travelling almost an hour to attend the sessions, a half-day observation schedule was not reasonable. Instead teachers were partnered with a school nearby and observations were made at two schools on each observation day. The curriculum consultant from the central office attended the first session to launch the project, and attended subsequent meetings when available.

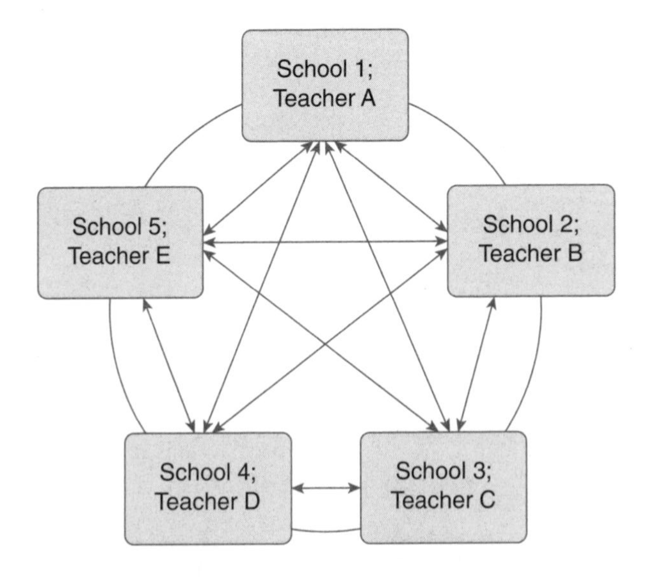

Figure 1.3 One Teacher/Multiple Schools

MEETING	PURPOSE	DATE
Networked Lab Class Meeting— held at one of the participating schools or central location	• Determine inquiry question • Establish schedule of observation visits	Late October Full day
Lab Class Observation—held at School A and B	• Observation at School A in the morning • Travel to school B • Lunch • Observation at School B	Late November Full Day
Lab Class Observation—held at School C and D	• Observation at School C in the morning • Travel to School D • Lunch • Observation at School D	Mid-December Full Day
Lab Class Observation—held at School E and F	• Observation at School E in the morning • Travel to School F • Lunch • Observation at School F	Late January Full Day
Lab Class Observation—held at School G and H	• Observation at School G in the morning • Travel to School H • Lunch • Observation at School H	Late February Full Day
Final Networked Lab Class Meeting—at one of the participating schools or central location	• Share student learning and professional learning • Classroom observation visit • Determine strategies for sharing the learning • Consolidation	Late March Full Day

Table 1.4 Overview of Lab Class—Potential Overall Schedule for One Teacher/Multiple Schools

Available for download at **resources.corwin.com/LabClass**

The Launch Meeting

> Learning . . . is not a solitary endeavor; rather, it needs to be a highly social one. It depends on continual discussion and demonstration. People learn by watching one another, seeing various ways of solving a single problem, sharing their different "takes" on a concept or struggle, and developing a common language with which to talk about their goals, their work, and their ways of monitoring their progress or diagnosing their difficulties. When teachers publicly display what they are thinking, they learn from one another, but they also learn through articulating their ideas, justifying their views, and making valid arguments.
>
> —Burney (2004)

At the Launch Meeting, teachers may be feeling uncertain if they have not previously participated in a model of professional learning such as Lab Class or Collaborative Inquiry. Taking some time at the beginning of the meeting to share the goals of Lab Class and an overview of the model that your group will be using will help reduce stress for participants. This is also an opportunity to address any questions or misconceptions about the Lab Class model. Facilitators may wish to remind participants that:

- Lab Class is a professional learning structure that is focused on student observing and analyzing student conversation, action, and product with a focus on improving student learning.
- Lab Class involves taking descriptive observations of student conversation, action, and product in each other's classrooms.
- Lab Class is an asset-oriented approach—all participants are careful to ensure work is framed in the positive.

Determine an Overall Focus for Lab Class

Whether your Lab Class Network consists of a few teachers at one school or many teachers spread over several schools in a district or districts, choosing one overall topic or focus for the Lab Class Network is an important starting point prior to beginning the work. Current initiatives at the federal, state, or district level may be a factor in selecting a focus for the Lab Class Network. In addition, Lab Class facilitators and/or organizers may want to consider sources of funding when selecting an overall focus. Schools and teachers should be informed of the area of focus in the invitation to Lab Class so that they can determine if this topic aligns with their school's needs as well as their own learning goals and priorities.

Some areas of focus used in past Lab Class Networks include:

- Student communication of thinking in mathematics
- Student writing—organization, supporting details
- Supporting English Language Learners
- Student-led inquiry learning
- Outdoor learning and self-regulation
- Oral language and vocabulary development

The focus should be broad enough to allow multiple entry points for teachers regardless of their teaching assignment. For example, a group of teachers in a kindergarten to Grade 12 school organized a Lab Class Network with a focus on student communication of mathematical thinking. The strategies used by the primary teachers and the expectations they had for their students were different than those used by the secondary teachers, but the common focus on student communication of thinking created opportunities for discussion across grades. Teachers of different grades explored strategies for communication including student use of math manipulatives and technology. The continuum of mathematics concepts and vocabulary across the grades became evident because teachers of the youngest students could see how ideas that began in primary grades evolved in later grades, and teachers of students in later grades could see where these foundational skills began in the primary grades.

Lab Class has enabled teachers in getting a better understanding of our students across the school. It has given us the time to work together as colleagues in a meaningful way that puts our students at the forefront of the conversation.

—*Teacher*

Narrow the Focus

Note: In Lab Class models with Multiple Teachers at Multiple Schools, narrowing the focus is done in school teams.

Once teachers have determined a focus for their Lab Class collaborative work, the next step is to narrow the focus. To do this, teachers triangulate data using Template A (see page 127) to independently reflect and record:

- *Student Capabilities*—In which areas do their students excel academically? What are their students' social and emotional strengths? What do they enjoy about school? In Lab Class, we work from an asset-stance and return to these student strengths throughout the project.
- *Student Areas for Growth*—Which academic expectations are a challenge for this group of students? What learning skills require further development for students to achieve greater academic success?
- *Professional Curiosities*—Within the broader topic that has been chosen as the focus for this Lab Class collaborative work, what professional curiosities do they have as an educator? How does this Lab Class focus align with other professional learning in which they are currently engaged or plan to engage in the future? (Ontario Ministry of Education, 2011a)

After each teacher has completed the template, facilitators provide a large chunk of time for sharing. In networks with more than one school, the sharing takes place in school teams. One at a time, each teacher shares their students' strengths while one teacher acts as recorder for the group. After all teachers are done sharing student strengths, the notes taken by the recorder are used to look for the commonalities shared by all participants about their students. All teachers then share their students' areas for growth, and again commonalities are noted. Last, teachers share their professional curiosities with the group and commonalities are noted.

Once teachers have determined common student strengths, areas for growth, and professional curiosities, they begin to draft their inquiry question using the frame: ***What is the impact of the instructional practice related to selected focus on the identified student learning need?*** The inquiry is phrased in the form of a question because "human beings tend to be more motivated to answer questions than to simply think about issues" (Katz & Dack, 2012). Rather than provide teachers with examples of inquiry questions, which may influence or limit their thinking, these criteria can guide teachers in evaluating and refining their inquiry question.

Good Inquiry Questions:

- Have deep impact on student learning and educator practice
- Generate deep thinking and value multiple perspectives
- Provoke action, dialogue, and reflection
- Are feasible regarding time, effort, and resources
- Are open-ended with many possible answers
- Are not based on a commercial resource
- Are inclusive of all educators involved
- Are something you are GENUINELY curious and passionate about
- Are worthy and rich enough to study and research
- Require the gathering and analysis of a variety of data over time

Adapted from Ministry of Education, Ontario, Canada

As teachers engage in Lab Class, the inquiry question may continue to evolve. Based on their observations of students and their reflections on their own professional learning, the inquiry question is revised as teachers rethink previously held beliefs and co-construct new understandings.

Sample: School Team Reflections Leading to Inquiry Questions

In the sample below, kindergarten to Grade 4 teachers from three different schools were interested in exploring the impact of inquiry-based learning on student learning and achievement. While all three schools had the same area of focus, their identified student capabilities, areas for growth, and professional curiosities led to unique inquiry questions for each school team.

SCHOOLS	CAPABILITIES	AREAS FOR GROWTH	PROFESSIONAL CURIOSITIES	INQUIRY QUESTION
First Street Public School	• Creative • Inquisitive • Feel safe taking risks • Confident in their areas of interest/passion • Good talkers	• Listening • Recording their thinking, esp. written tasks • Articulating their thinking focused on the task • Self-regulation	• How to meaningfully engage in inquiry across the curriculum • How to run "Knowledge Building Circles"—brainstorm connector statements	What is the impact of intentionally creating an inquiry learning environment that provokes student action, dialogue, and reflection on students' expression of their learning?

SCHOOLS	CAPABILITIES	AREAS FOR GROWTH	PROFESSIONAL CURIOSITIES	INQUIRY QUESTION
	• Maintain focus	• Problem-solving strategies across content areas	• Back-mapping curriculum expectations • How to nudge and/or push kids forward with their inquiry	
Second Street Public School	• Excited about learning; inquisitive • Love school and learning • Positive attitude about school in general	• Responsibility and accountability to the classroom community • Students sometimes lack confidence; don't see themselves as learners • Oral communication skills are an area of concern	• Where and when does inquiry end? Does it have to end? • Parent education and student expectations around what is learning? What is homework? • Reporting and assessment	What is the impact of explicitly teaching oral language on students' confidence and ability to express their thoughts, ideas, and questions within an inquiry-based environment?
Third Street Public School	• Hands on • Naturally curious • Drawn to natural environment • Some want to ask questions • Maintain focus when engaged in inquiry • Beginning to self-regulate	• Asking deeper questions • Explaining thinking more fully • Respectfully challenging and defending ideas • Building community's knowledge	• How to set up a safe learning environment where students feel safe to take risks • How to model asking deeper questions • How to build community knowledge • When are educator moves necessary • How to use documentation • Pausing, reflecting, and asking why before judging (growth mind set)	What is the impact of responsive educator actions on students' ability to demonstrate their critical thinking?

Additional Examples

Example One: Math Problem Solving

STUDENT CAPABILITIES	AREAS FOR GROWTH	PROFESSIONAL CURIOSITIES	INQUIRY QUESTION
• Enjoy mathematics • Can read the problems • Work well with partners	• Math vocabulary • Conceptual understanding of mathematics	• How do students make sense of math problems? • Why are they struggling to solve math problems? • Why do they not seem to know where to start?	What is the impact of an increased focus on the explicit teaching of mathematical concepts on students' ability to understand and work through math problems?

Link to Common Core Standards:

CCSS.Math.Practice.MP1 Make sense of problems and persevere in solving them.

Example Two: Research Writing

STUDENT CAPABILITIES	AREAS FOR GROWTH	PROFESSIONAL CURIOSITIES	INQUIRY QUESTION
Comfortable using technology to find information	• Need more awareness of a variety of nonfiction resources • Supporting their ideas with facts and research • Understanding how to execute the steps of the research process	• How do we help students critically examine information? • How do we help students present their arguments and research coherently?	How does the strategic teaching of the research process using a variety of technologies impact the writing process and the understanding of nonfiction texts?

Link to Common Core Standards:

CCSS.ELA-LITERACY.W4.2 Write informative/explanatory texts to examine a topic and convey ideas and information clearly.

CCSS.ELA-LITERACY.W.4.2B Develop the topic with facts, definitions, concrete details, quotations, or other information and examples related to the topic.

CCSS.ELA-LITERACY.WHST.6-8.1 Write arguments focused on discipline-specific content.

CCSS.ELA-LITERACY.WHST.6-8.1.B Support claim(s) with logical reasoning and relevant, accurate data and evidence that demonstrate an understanding of the topic or text, using credible sources.

Theories of Action

A theory of action describes the actions and ideas we have about how to achieve a goal. Surprisingly, teachers may have two different theories of action: their *espoused theory* that encompasses their beliefs, attitudes, and values, and their *theory in use*, which is the theory that they use in their practice (Argyris, 1995).

Lee (2009, cited in Donohoo, 2013) shared examples of teachers' differing espoused theories and theories in use.

1. Teachers believed that good writing was more than simply form, but they provided most of their feedback in that category.
2. Teachers believed it was best to focus feedback on specific errors or feedback for a specific purpose, but they marked errors comprehensively.
3. Teachers believed that students would benefit from locating and correcting their own errors, but they consistently corrected and located errors for students.
4. Teachers believed that students had limited ability to decipher editing codes, but they used them anyway.
5. Teachers believed that scores or grades caused students to ignore teacher feedback, but they gave them anyway.
6. Teachers believed it was important to highlight students' strengths and weaknesses, but they focused on the weaknesses.
7. Teachers believed that students should take more responsibility for their learning, but their practices took this control away from students, making it nearly impossible.
8. Teachers believed that the writing process was helpful, but teachers asked the students to write single drafts and provided feedback on these, responding to the product at the end instead of providing feedback throughout the process.
9. Teachers believed that students would continue to make the errors that the teacher corrected in their work, but teachers continued to focus on correcting student errors.
10. Teachers believed that the effort they invested in providing students with feedback was ineffective but they did not alter their feedback practices.

During the Launch Meeting, it is important that teachers take time to articulate their theories of action and the underlying assumptions that form the foundation for their theories. It is by bringing these beliefs and assumptions to the forefront that we can confront any inconsistencies between their espoused theories of action and their theories in use.

Argyris (1995) notes that individuals are often unaware of the inconsistency between their espoused theories and theories of action, and furthermore, organizations develop defensive routines, policies, and practices that protect organizational participants from embarrassment or threat. These protective measures reinforce the theories in use and create a barrier to learning for both the individual and the organization.

Additionally, theories in use often exist below the conscious level. Teachers have internalized their theories in use, and these beliefs and actions are routine and automatic. Asking teachers to dig deep and unpack their underlying theories in use can be uncomfortable and difficult, but it is noticing and examining these inconsistencies that creates opportunities for professional learning.

It can be helpful to use analogies to illustrate inconsistencies between people's espoused theories and their theories in use. My beliefs about healthy eating would include statements like:

- Meals should include lots of vegetables and small portions of lean protein and starch.
- Eating a healthy breakfast is important.
- Processed and packaged foods should be consumed in moderation.
- Sweets and junk food should be eaten rarely.

These could be shared as theories of action using if–then statements:

- If my meals include lots of vegetables and small portions of lean protein and starches, then I will attain the necessary vitamins and minerals required for good health.
- If I eat a healthy breakfast, then my body and brain will have the fuel I need to be productive.
- If I reduce the amount of packaged and processed foods I consume, then I will reduce my intake of sodium.
- If I avoid sweets and junk food, then my body will not convert extra calories to fat and store that fat on my body.

However, my actual theories in use would be:

- If I eat a healthy salad for lunch, then I can splurge at dinner.
- If I went to the gym and worked out, then I can eat some junk food guilt free.
- If I eat organic crackers and chips, then they are a healthy snack not a processed food.

The first two are the types of rationalizations that we often make and, deep down, know that they do not align with our espoused theories. But the third statement is one where we might be challenging some existing beliefs and we may need to do more research and confront the inconsistencies. If we are trying to reduce the amount of processed and packaged foods in our diet, then do organic packaged and processed foods count as healthy or unhealthy?

Below are the theories of action developed during our Launch Meeting with the kindergarten to Grade 4 teams from the three schools described earlier in this chapter. First Street Public School provides us with an interesting example of theories in use and theories in action. Initially they identified the students' inability to ask higher order thinking questions as an area on which to focus. The teachers shared examples from their practice including a teacher who described a provocation she used to elicit higher order thinking questions from her Grade 1 students. "I brought in all different kinds of pumpkins in October—big, small, short and fat, tall and skinny, some were bumpy, some were smooth, some were white, most were orange. I thought the pumpkins would spark some science inquiry around plants, growing things, or fall. I brought the pumpkins to the carpet for our group time and asked the students if they had any questions, any wonderings about the pumpkins. Nothing! No one had any questions. How can I do inquiry learning if they don't have any questions?"

The teachers at First Street Public School used scaffolded learning in other curriculum areas, and their espoused theories and theories in use for literacy were well aligned. They included the beliefs:

- If teachers scaffold learning to read through modeled, shared, and guided reading, then students will acquire the skills and ability to read independently.
- If teachers scaffold learning to write through modeled, shared, and guided writing, then students will acquire the skills and ability to write independently.
- If teachers provide small group instruction of specific reading strategies to purposefully chosen groups of three to five students, students will expand their repertoire of reading strategies.

Their espoused theory for their inquiry-based science program was, "If teachers scaffold inquiry-learning through modeling and small group instruction, then students will acquire the skills and abilities to engage in inquiry." They had identified *students' ability to ask higher order questions* as one of the skills that were required for successful inquiry-based learning, but the scaffolding that was so evident in their literacy instruction was missing. The teacher brought in the pumpkins and expected that the students would be able to ask questions. They realized their theory in use was "If teachers provide interesting provocations, students will be able to ask higher order questions."

The teachers recognized if they wanted the students to demonstrate the skill of asking higher order questions, then they had to teach the students that skill using the same techniques that they used to scaffold learning of reading skills. Suddenly the problem went from "the students don't ask questions" to "we haven't taught them how to ask questions!" The inconsistency between their espoused theory and their theory in use was now so obvious that the path forward became much clearer. Instead of thinking of bigger and better provocations, they needed to explicitly teach the students how to ask higher order questions.

SCHOOLS	INQUIRY QUESTION	THEORIES OF ACTION
First Street Public School	What is the impact of intentionally creating an inquiry learning environment that provokes student action, dialogue, and reflection on students' expression of their learning?	• If a provocation space or station were made available in the classroom, then students will ask higher order questions. • If higher order questions are modeled and explicitly taught, then students will ask higher order questions of each other. • If higher level question stems are generated, practiced, and posted, then students will ask higher level questions. • If educators collaborate to brainstorm ongoing provocations to expand existing inquiries, then students will produce higher level responses. • If educators use novel materials, texts, and learning opportunities linked to curriculum to provoke inquiry, then students will demonstrate curricular expectations in expressions of their learning. • If educators monitor student interest in learning opportunities and aim to maintain this interest, then students will demonstrate increased knowledge in expressions of their learning. • If educators follow student interests, then students' stamina will increase
Second Street Public School	What is the impact of explicitly teaching oral language on students' confidence and ability to express their thoughts, ideas, and questions within an inquiry-based environment?	• If students are explicitly taught to reflect and think critically about their ideas, thoughts, and questions, then they will see the value of their ideas and have the confidence to share their ideas with others. • If teachers provide students with multiple and varied opportunities to share their reflections and observations of their learning with others, then they will see themselves as effective communicators. • If teachers provide students with multiple and varied opportunities to share their reflections and observations of their learning with others, then they will engage more effectively as learners.

SCHOOLS	INQUIRY QUESTION	THEORIES OF ACTION
Third Street Public School	What is the impact of responsive educator actions on students' ability to demonstrate their critical thinking?	• If all students know they are valued, then a sense of community will be developed. • If student voice is considered, then students will take more ownership of their learning. • If documentation is purposeful, then it will provide assessment for learning to uncover students' strengths, needs, and interests. • If authentic learning experiences are created then students will engage in a deeper level in their learning.

Additional Examples

Example One: Math Problem Solving

STUDENT CAPABILITIES	INQUIRY QUESTION	THEORIES OF ACTION
Enjoy mathematics Can read the problems Work well with partners	What is the impact of an increased focus on the explicit teaching of mathematical concepts on students' ability to understand and work through math problems?	• If students have opportunities to share their thinking with others, then they will use math vocabulary to demonstrate conceptual understanding. • If students have opportunities to demonstrate conceptual understanding through a variety of problem-solving strategies, then staff can identify the students' current conceptual understanding. • If staff understand students' current conceptual understandings (through student work, conversations, observations) then it will inform their instruction.

At first, teachers thought that students were struggling with math problem solving because they lacked the math vocabulary to understand the problems. Through observation and conversation with students, teachers noticed that students didn't understand the math concepts within the math problems. Also, the teachers noticed that the current problem-solving model that they were using didn't always allow student thinking to emerge. The theories of action they created include creating opportunities for students to use alternative strategies, models, and procedures to demonstrate their understanding and problem solving.

Link to Common Core Standards:

CCSS.Math.Practice.MP1 Make sense of problems and persevere in solving them.

Example Two: Research Writing

STUDENT CAPABILITIES	INQUIRY QUESTION	THEORIES OF ACTION
Comfortable using technology to find information	How does the strategic teaching of the research process using a variety of technologies impact the writing process and the understanding of nonfiction texts?	• If teachers explicitly teach the research process steps, then students will be able to research a topic of interest independently. • If students have access to a range of technology for their research, then they will be engaged in finding and recording information that supports their ideas or is related to their topic. • If the steps of the research process are "chunked" for students, then students will be able to track their progress to project completion.

Teachers noticed that students were very comfortable using the Internet to research topics for writing projects but were uncertain about what to do with all the information they gathered. They didn't know how to organize their research process.

Link to Common Core Standards:

CCSS.ELA-LITERACY.W4.2 Write informative/explanatory texts to examine a topic and convey ideas and information clearly.

CCSS.ELA-LITERACY.W.4.2B Develop the topic with facts, definitions, concrete details, quotations, or other information and examples related to the topic.

CCSS.ELA-LITERACY.WHST.6-8.1 Write arguments focused on discipline-specific content.

CCSS.ELA-LITERACY.WHST.6-8.1.B Support claim(s) with logical reasoning and relevant, accurate data and evidence that demonstrate an understanding of the topic or text, using credible sources.

Learn to Be Descriptive

For many teachers, it becomes second nature to observe students and then immediately begin to determine what they have learned and understood, what are the student's next steps for learning, and what are our next steps for teaching. City, Elmore, Fiarman, and Teitel (2011) noted that trying to simply observe what we see at the most basic descriptive level without inference or judgement is very challenging, and we have experienced this in working with educators, new and experienced, from all grade levels. To ensure that teachers can engage in descriptive observations during their classroom visits, we take a large chunk of time to practice this skill during the Launch Meeting.

Descriptive Observations Using Photographs

To begin, participants engage in descriptive observation as a large group. Using a data projector, document camera, or other device, the facilitator displays a photograph of an adult or child engaged in an activity and invites participants to describe what they see. If someone offers an observation that is a judgement or an inference, the facilitator or another participant can ask for clarification, "How do you know?" Some statements are obvious inferences such as, "He seems happy" or "She likes to play with the blocks," while others are more subtle. For example, we used a photograph of a firefighter sitting on a curb, resting his or her head on their knees, with a burning building in the background. A participant started his observation with, "I see a firefighter . . . ," and another participant said, "How do you know it's a firefighter? It could be an actor, and this is a scene from a show." So the participant revised his observation and said, "I see an adult wearing a white helmet, big yellow coat and pants, and large black rubber boots with a white stripe . . ." After the initial sharing, facilitators may probe deeper, asking, "What else do you notice?" to prompt participants to notice some of the details in the photograph.

Next, participants repeat this activity with a partner. Each person receives a photograph in a folder. Again, facilitators can use photographs from Google Images of people engaged in various activities, both indoors and outside, or classroom photos. Be sure to use photographs and not graphic illustrations or clip art so that participants can transfer their learning to photo documentation from their classroom. Partner A, keeping the photo hidden inside the folder, describes the scene in the photograph to Partner B using only descriptive language. If Partner B hears something they think has moved beyond description and into judgement or inference, they can challenge Partner A. Once Partner A is finished describing the photograph, they ask Partner B if they have a picture in their mind of the scene that they have described. When Partner B is ready, Partner A reveals the scene and the two of them discuss any discrepancies between what Partner A described and what Partner B was visualizing. What might have caused this discrepancy? What language could Partner A have used that would have made this clearer? Then it is Partner B's turn to describe their photograph to Partner A and repeat the process.

Once both Partner A and Partner B have had a turn to engage in this activity, the facilitator can debrief the whole group. What did participants find challenging about this activity? What strategies did they use to try to remain in a descriptive stance and to refrain from inference or judgement? When and how might this skill of descriptive observation be useful to them as a classroom teacher?

Last, educators engage in descriptive observation using a short video clip of students in action. In this video clip, three kindergarten students are engaged in a discussion about "the real alphabet." Participants work in triads, each one choosing one of the three students to observe and recording their observations on their chosen student. Following the video, participants can regroup with those who observed the same student and share their observations, noting any inferences or judgements. Then they can regroup into their original triad and share again.

To view the video, go to: http://thelearningexchange.ca/kto2connection/Module_3_K-2_Connections/Module_3_K-2_Connections.htm.

Click on Literacy & Math Learning and select the video for Alphabet Investigation.

As a large group or in smaller groups, the participants can sort these observation cards into descriptive observations and not descriptive observations.

Boy: "It is the real one, right Ms. Lauren?"	The girl can debate with her peers.
The boy is frustrated because the other children won't listen to him when he tells them all the letters are real.	Girl: "Take a good look. What's different about this?" She points to letters.
The girl recognizes the characteristics of letters.	Teacher asks the girl, "Why did you bring that here?" Girl: "To show Caleb it's the same."
Boy: "Guys, how many times do I have to say this. They are all real. They actually are real. I'm not kidding."	The boy wants the teacher to tell the other students that he is right.
The blonde boy does not know all his letters.	Girl: "The only thing that's different is that these have flat parts and these ones don't." She points to the W on the paper and on the alphabet card.

Other videos that are more relevant to the teachers can be selected by the facilitator.

Grade 12 Math Student Problem Solving 2: http://thelearningexchange.ca/projects/math-conversations-that-count-grades-1-to-12/?p-cat=999&sess=4

I am excited to see that Lab Class has shifted the focus of our learning and the way we do things during our school-based learning sessions. Our learning and understanding comes from sitting with, observing, and talking with our students. The descriptive observations we make allow us to make informed decisions regarding our students' strengths and our students' learning needs.

—Principal

Lab Class Simulation

The facilitator leads the group through a mock Lab Class experience using the observations of the video in the same way that teachers will use their observations from a Lab Class classroom observation visit. Returning to the Alphabet Investigation video, let's assume the inquiry question is: "What is the impact of various font and text explorations on students' understanding of letters and ability to read words?" First, ask each participant to sort their observations—which ones relate to the inquiry question and which ones do not? Once they have narrowed down their observations, each teacher should select up to three of their observations related to the question and record each observation on a separate sticky note. Invite one teacher to share an observation and post it on the wall or other area. Invite other teachers to share similar observations. For example, one teacher may share an observation that a student is pointing to the letters on the alphabet card as they speak. Other teachers may share the same or similar observations about how the children use the alphabet cards.

Once all the observations related to the use of the alphabet cards are posted, the teachers can be invited to create a heading for this group. What does this group of observations tell us in relation to the inquiry question and/or the learning conditions in the classroom? One possible heading might be "student use of classroom resources" or "student access to classroom resources." The remaining observations recorded on sticky notes are sorted as teachers continue to identify emerging trends and note the conditions present that allowed those trends to emerge. This process is described in greater detail in Chapter 3.

Select Marker Students

In their daily practice, teachers observe and document the learning of all students, but for Lab Class we ask teachers to select three or four marker students to monitor and observe throughout the inquiry process. Marker students are also called "students of mystery" because they are able to achieve and yet they are not, and there is no observable reason for their lack of progress (Ontario Ministry of Education, 2012, 2015). Keeping the inquiry question in mind, teachers select marker students who they expect will most likely be impacted by the instructional strategy or strategies chosen. Marker students can be representative of a small group of students in the classroom. For example, if one of the selected marker students is an English Language Learner (ELL), then the teachers' in-depth observations of and conversations with this student may inform his or her practice with other ELL students in the class.

Considerations for choosing marker students could include:

- Do they represent a group of students in the class?
- Is the student need chosen for the Lab Class inquiry question an area of growth for this student?
- Is it unclear why the student is underperforming?
- Are we unsure how this student learns best?
- Is this student able to share their thinking and learning, either verbally or nonverbally?

Document Student Learning

Once the marker students have been selected, teachers need to consider what evidence they want to collect, what strategies and tools they will use to document their observations of student learning, conversations with students, and student work (Ontario Ministry of Education, 2015). This triangulation of data is very important to ensure that we have a clear picture of each student's learning and growth. If we use only our observations or only samples of student work, we may not have a complete picture of the child's learning.

In this example, a teacher observed a Grade 5 student while he was working on a subtraction question. She copied the numbers as the student wrote them and then recorded their conversation. While the written work seems to indicate the student can follow the procedure for subtraction with regrouping, the conversation reveals several misconceptions in his understanding.

Work sample:

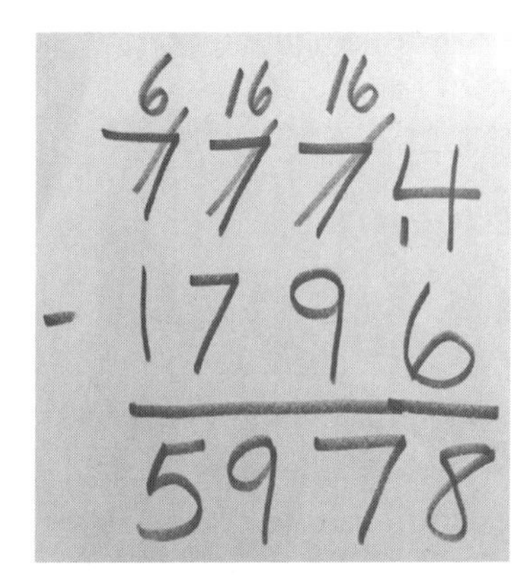

Figure 2.1

Conversation:

Teacher: Talk to me about this question. Can you tell me how you got your answer?

Student looks at the teacher. His facial expression makes her wonder if he is unsure of the question or unsure what to say.

Teacher: What number did you start with?

Student: Four subtract six.

Teacher: And?

Student: Oh, fourteen.

Teacher: And how did you get fourteen?

Student: I crossed out the seven and (pause)

Teacher: What happened when you crossed out the seven?

Student:	I put the one beside the four.
Teacher:	Why? Why didn't you just do four subtract six?
Student:	It wouldn't work.
Teacher:	Why?
Student:	Because if you had four subtract six would be zero.
Teacher:	What happens when you cross out your seven? You crossed out seven, put a six, and put a one in front of the four. What happens when you do that?
Student:	Ummm. (pause)
Teacher:	Is that just something you're used to doing?
Student:	Yah.
Teacher:	So you have fourteen subtract six equals eight. Then what did you do?
Student:	Cross out the other seven. Put the one beside the six.
Teacher:	When you're putting the one beside the six what's happening?
Student:	You're rounding.

Teachers may choose from a wide range of strategies for documenting student learning including photographs, video, collection of student work samples, interviews, conversations, and student reflections and self-evaluations. Each teacher can choose the documentation strategies that they wish; it is not necessary for everyone to be using the same documentation strategies. During the Launch Meeting, teachers can use Template C (see page 129) to plan their student data collection. This plan may change as the Lab Class progresses over time, but it is important for teachers to commit to an initial plan for documentation.

Document Teacher Learning

While many teachers are experienced at documenting student learning, they may have little or no experience documenting their own professional learning and growth. In our early Lab Class projects, each participant was provided with a journal and was asked to use the journal to record their thoughts, observations, and reflections about the Lab Class process and their own professional learning. While some participants found this to be a useful strategy, other teachers expressed their dislike of journals as a method of documenting their thinking. In subsequent sessions, teachers were encouraged to use a range of methods for documenting their professional learning and growth. Some teachers chose to journal using a word processing program; others chose a traditional written journal; while others used audio recordings, photos, and visual arts to represent their learning. Teachers can use Template D (see page 130) to create a plan for collecting evidence of their own professional learning.

Template C

Data Collection for Student Learning

INQUIRY QUESTION:
What does the impact of an increased focus on the explicit teaching of mathematical concepts have on students' ability to understand and solve math problems?

WHAT EVIDENCE WILL BE COLLECTED?	HOW?	WHEN? BY WHOM?
Evidence: • Samples of marker students' math problem-solving work • Interviews with marker students	• Collection of student work • Create interview questions with Lab Class group • Meet briefly with individual marker students during math class • Record their answers on paper and using iPad audio recording	• Weekly; collected by teacher • In January (beginning of Lab Class) and again in May (end of Lab Class)

Template D

Data Collection for Teacher Reflection and Professional Learning

INQUIRY QUESTION:
What is the impact of an increased focus on the explicit teaching of mathematical concepts on students' ability to understand and work through math problems?

WHAT EVIDENCE WILL BE COLLECTED?	HOW?	WHEN? BY WHOM?
Evidence: List of mathematical concepts explicitly taught—whole class and small group	Create a T-chart—date, concept, instruction method—and keep in my daybook or posted near my desk	Collected by teachers—ongoing

Facilitators should set aside time during each Lab Class meeting for teachers to document their learning to ensure that this documentation takes place throughout the journey. Just as it is powerful to look back to see how far our students have come in their learning, it is equally powerful to reflect on our own learning and growth as professionals. Also, like our student data, it is important to triangulate data on teacher learning. In addition to the reflections recorded by the teachers, facilitators can collect their own data through observations and conversations with teachers and administrators participating in Lab Class. This triangulation of data can be used by facilitators to develop a more accurate picture of teacher and student learning during Lab Class.

During one Lab Class project, a team of teachers from one school was researching "What is the impact of integrating the Arts on student achievement in reading, specifically on: making connections, making inferences, expressing personal thoughts and feelings about what has been read, and identifying the point of view of the speaker in a piece of text and suggesting possible alternative perspective?" (Teachers could differentiate by selecting specific art strands—visual arts, drama, dance, or music—based on student need and interest. Teachers could choose to focus on reading skills depending on the strengths and needs of their students.)

Link to Common Core Standards:

CCSS.ELA-LITERACY.CCRA.R.1 Read closely to determine what the text says explicitly and to make logical inferences from it; cite specific textual evidence when writing or speaking to support conclusions drawn from the text.

CCSS.ELA-LITERACY.CCRA.R.6 Assess how point of view or purpose shapes the content and style of a text.

CCSS.ELA-LITERACY.CCRA.R.9 Analyze how two or more texts address similar themes or topics to build knowledge or to compare the approaches the authors take.

Teachers completed a survey prior to beginning Lab Class and at the culminating meeting at the end of Lab Class. (Survey questions adapted from Oreck, B. [2004].) While the post-survey results indicated some improvement in teachers' confidence and ability to integrate the arts into the curriculum, the results didn't reflect the enthusiasm expressed by teachers in conversations, the excitement observed during classroom visits, and the comments in the teachers' written reflection journals. Only by considering a wider range of data did a more accurate view of teacher learning become evident. The question responses and comments below are a sample, taken from four teachers' written reflections at our culminating meeting.

Question 2: I feel confident in my ability to facilitate drama activities.

PRETEST N=9 POSTTEST N=10	STRONGLY AGREE	AGREE	DISAGREE	STRONGLY DISAGREE
Pretest Response % Response Count	11.1 1	55.6 5	22.2 2	11.1 1
Posttest Response % Response Count	0.0 0	90.0 9	10.0 1	0.0 0

Question 4: I feel confident in my ability to facilitate music activities.

PRETEST N=9 POSTTEST N=10	STRONGLY AGREE	AGREE	DISAGREE	STRONGLY DISAGREE
Pretest Response % Response Count	11.1 1	44.4 4	22.2 2	22.2 2
Posttest Response % Response Count	10.0 1	40.0 4	40.0 4	10.0 1

Question 5: I feel confident in my ability to facilitate visual arts activities.

PRETEST N=9 POSTTEST N=10	STRONGLY AGREE	AGREE	DISAGREE	STRONGLY DISAGREE
Pretest Response % Response Count	11.1 1	66.7 6	11.1 1	11.1 1
Posttest Response % Response Count	40.0 4	50.0 5	10.0 1	0.0 0

Question 6: I feel that I don't have enough time to teach the arts along with the rest of the curriculum.

PRETEST N=9 POSTTEST N=10	STRONGLY AGREE	AGREE	DISAGREE	STRONGLY DISAGREE
Pretest Response % Response Count	22.2 2	22.2 2	44.4 4	11.1 1
Posttest Response % Response Count	0.0 0	50.0 5	50.0 5	0.0 0

Question 8: I feel that I have enough resources to incorporate the arts into my classroom.

PRETEST N=9 POSTTEST N=10	STRONGLY AGREE	AGREE	DISAGREE	STRONGLY DISAGREE
Pretest Response % Response Count	11.1 1	33.3 3	44.4 4	11.1 1
Posttest Response % Response Count	10.0 1	40.0 4	50.0 5	0.0

Question 9: I feel that many students in my class would benefit from more arts activities in the curriculum.

PRETEST N=9 POSTTEST N=10	STRONGLY AGREE	AGREE	DISAGREE	STRONGLY DISAGREE
Pretest Response % Response Count	33.3 3	66.7 6	0.0 0	0.0 0
Posttest Response % Response Count	40.0 4	60.0 6	0.0 0	0.0 0

Survey questions adapted from Oreck, (2004).

Teacher A: I am a visual and kinesthetic learner and require that hands-on approach. One key piece of learning from this inquiry is that I looked at teaching and learning in a whole new way. I feel that the arts are a valuable part of students' learning and should be taught more often in a cross-curricular way.

Teacher B: Now I actually know about the professional resources available in my building. In addition, I have been given and shown and participated in some practical art and drama activities throughout the course of this inquiry. The handbook (from the university students) will be a great tool for further arts lessons. One key piece of learning is the results we have seen—the students' ability to respond has increased.

Teacher C: I learned about how the arts complement the curriculum. The importance of including the arts into other areas of the curriculum not only benefits the students' learning, but it motivates them as well. They seem to be very engaged in arts activities, and when it is connected to literacy there is a higher percentage of comprehension.

Having a range of data including the written reflections and survey results from the teachers, as well as our own notes from observations and conversations, gave us a much more comprehensive understanding of the teacher and student learning that had occurred during this Lab Class. A complete summary of this Lab Class project is available in Chapter 5.

Ethical Considerations When Documenting Student and Teacher Learning

As teachers move forward with Lab Class, we must consider ethical issues around documenting student learning and student consent (Ontario Ministry of Education, 2013). Loris Malaguzzi (1994) believed that "[w]hen the child is observed, the child is happy—it's almost an honor that he is observed by an adult." Pedagogical documentation is a foundation of the Reggio Emilia approach to education that he helped found. Yet Pat Tarr (2011) cautioned educators that

> what it means for children to give informed consent is shifting as researchers devise ways to make their research objectives, the use of the data collected, the specifics of what is required of the children and their right to withdraw at any time understandable—even to very young children. We might openly discuss and ask for consent from children before we begin to document, and to consider that this is provisional consent that is continually renegotiated. (p. 15)

While teachers can choose whether or not to participate in Lab Class, their students don't usually have a voice or choice in that decision. When other teachers and administrators are coming in to observe students, how do we ensure the students have a voice in the documentation process? Facilitators need to consider how to continuously renegotiate consent with educators and students as they engage in learning together. While we may believe that we have been considerate of educators' and students' thoughts, ideas, and feelings, it is imperative that we dig deeper and uncover the ethical dilemmas inherent in our work.

One strategy that we found effective with all age groups of students was to explain to them the purpose of the Lab Class teacher observations on the day of the observation and ask them if they were willing to share their learning with the observers. Each teacher whose class was being observed that day explained to their students that watching students work and talking to students helped teachers understand how students were learning and that those observations were going to help us try to be better teachers. Students could select a sticker to wear "Yes, I'd like to share" or "No, thank you." All students were required to participate in the learning, just as they would any other day; however, they could choose whether or not they wanted to share their learning with the observing teachers.

Once we began documenting student learning during a visit, we always asked permission from the student(s) before photographing or videotaping their work. We found that students who had initially chosen a "No, thank you" sticker traded it for a "Yes, I'd like to share sticker" once the visit began. During one visit a student asked the teacher, "Are those the teachers who are here to learn from us?" When the teacher answered yes, the student replied, "Excuse me, I have to go share my thinking with them." On visits to schools that were participating in Lab Class, teachers have had students ask them in the hallway, "Are you coming to our class so we can share our learning?" One Grade 3 student was being observed during a math problem-solving activity, and she was explaining her thinking to the observing teacher. "Wow, that's a really interesting strategy," the teacher remarked. "Aren't you going to write it down?" the student replied. The students became active participants in Lab Class during these classroom observation visits.

Those educators who consent to lead and/or participate in capacity building in their school or at a system level should know how the learning will be shared and with whom. Orb, Eisenhauer, and Wynaden (2000) suggest that participants give their consent for use of quotations in publications and reports. School districts who received funding were required to write a ministry report (see Chapter 5 for samples of these reports). Initially, the reports were written by the facilitators and then submitted to the ministry, with copies sent to the administrators at the schools that participated to be shared with the teachers. Upon reflection, we realized that the documentation of teacher learning and the final report to the district and the ministry needed to be much more collaborative. If the learning is collaborative, then the reporting should be collaborative, too. In subsequent years, participants were informed at the first meeting that the group would be working together to prepare a final report for the ministry at the end of the year. Each time teachers met, observations, conversations and teacher comments were collected to document our learning as a group. Each time, teachers were informed that this documentation may be used for the final report (see Templates E, F, and G). At the final meeting, the group created the outline for the ministry report together. The facilitator then took all the ideas and put them together in a final document, which was shared again with all members of the group for final input before being submitted. Like students, teachers were excited to share their learning with the ministry. Often they would arrive with notes and photos for sharing and tell the facilitators, "Make sure you tell the ministry . . ."

Create and Discuss Norms

To work effectively as a group, participants must share ideas, take turns, disagree with and listen to others, and generate and reconcile points of view (Blumenfeld, Marx, Soloway, & Krajcik, 1996). Teachers frequently work alone in their classroom, and putting them together as a group does not guarantee that they will be able to learn together cooperatively. As a group, it is important that the participants create the norms for the in-class observation visits. These are recorded and then reviewed before each classroom observation visit. The norms can be revised as needed during the Lab Class process. During Lab Class, one group of teachers reported that they found it stressful when participants were talking in the hallway on the way back to the meeting area after the classroom observation. They were concerned that the other participants were sharing their observations ahead of time and that as the observed teacher they wanted the participants to wait and share when everyone could hear their observations. As a result, the group added the norm "Minimize hallway conversations" to their list.

Some examples of norms:

- Be positive. Focus on student assets and competencies.
- Record observations of student conversations, actions, and products.
- Observe silently for at least 10 minutes before asking students any questions, unless the students engage with you.
- Ensure any questions asked of teachers and students are open-ended.
- Minimize hallway conversations.

Establish the Schedule for Lab Class

The final task at the Launch Meeting, now that all participants are aware of what this learning model involves and what their role will be, is to create the schedule for the remainder of the sessions and to determine who will be hosting observation visits at each session. The actual number of classroom observation visits and Networked Meetings may vary depending on the number of participants, the number of schools, and the budget for release time. The finalized schedule should be shared electronically with all participants, including the school administrator, at the end of the Launch Meeting. If the team would like the support of other district personnel or community agencies, they may also take this time to invite them to subsequent meetings for support.

The schedules shared below were developed over many years of Lab Class with groups ranging from six teachers at one school to a group of 32 teachers from four different schools. If the Launch Meeting is done during the time usually allotted for school-based PLCs, the Launch Meeting may take multiple days.

Possible Launch Class Schedule: Full Day Release

TOPIC	SUGGESTED TIME ALLOTMENT (MAY VARY DEPENDING ON THE GROUP)
Introduction: What Is Lab Class? Overview and Expectations	15 minutes
Determine a Focus (may be determined in advance)	15 minutes
Narrow the Focus Develop an Inquiry Question and Theories of Action	30 minutes 30 minutes
Learn to Be Descriptive	60 minutes
Lab Class Simulation	30 minutes
Select Marker Students Documenting Learning: Students and Teachers	30 minutes
Create Norms	15 minutes
Planning and Scheduling	25 minutes
Feedback; Q & A	10 minutes

Possible Launch Meetings Schedule: PLC Model (100-minute block)

TOPIC	SUGGESTED TIME ALLOTMENT (MAY VARY DEPENDING ON THE GROUP)
Introduction: What Is Lab Class? Overview and Expectations	15 minutes
Determine a Focus (done in advance)	
Narrow the Focus Develop an Inquiry Question and Theories of Action	45 minutes
Learn to Be Descriptive	40 minutes

Meeting One

TOPIC	SUGGESTED TIME ALLOTMENT (MAY VARY DEPENDING ON THE GROUP)
Review of Meeting One	10 minutes
Lab Class Simulation	20 minutes
Select Marker Students Documenting Learning: Students and Teachers	30 minutes
Create Norms	15 minutes
Planning and Scheduling	15 minutes
Feedback; Q & A	10 minutes

Meeting Two

Available for download at **resources.corwin.com/LabClass**

Troubleshooting Tips

Drafting an Inquiry Question

Some problems may arise when drafting the inquiry question including but not limited to

- Questions that do not fall within the teachers' agency
- Student learning needs identified that are not linked to curriculum standards or expectations
- Student learning needs identified that are challenging to measure

Using the frame of "What is the impact of *instructional practice* on *identified student learning need*?" as well as the guiding questions on Template B (see page 128) and the information from Template A can help teachers create an effective inquiry question. However, sometimes additional support and scaffolding from the facilitator may be needed.

Focusing on instructional practices steers teachers away from problems that may not fall within their own agency. One group of teachers had identified lack of parental involvement and few books at home as an issue impacting student reading achievement. The question stem helped them consider what instructional practices they could use that helped address areas of specific concern in reading achievement while moving the discussion of how to engage with parents to separate conversation. While parent engagement is important, Lab Class may not be the best model to address this issue.

Occasionally teachers have selected an area of student learning that is not part of the curriculum standards or expectations at the district, state, or national level. This does not happen very often and is usually remedied by asking teachers where the learning need fits in the curriculum. If it does not, then they may need to expand the scope of their inquiry. A group of Grade 2 to Grade 6 teachers had identified several challenges that their students were having with writing including organizing their thoughts and adding detail (CCSS.ELA.LITERACY 3.2 & 3.3). The conversation had evolved into a discussion on the importance of cursive writing, and they had created the inquiry question, "What is the impact of explicitly teaching cursive writing on students' achievement in writing?" With prompting from the facilitator, they went back and looked at the initial student needs—organization and adding detail. They realized their instructional strategy did not address those needs and was not linked to the curriculum. After more discussion, they revised the question to "What is the impact of using mentor texts on students' ability to organize their writing?"

On more than one occasion teachers have selected student engagement as the student learning need. The challenge becomes how do we define student engagement and how do we measure it? Returning to curriculum standards and expectations can be an effective strategy when teachers have selected a student learning need that is difficult to measure such as engagement or motivation. Another strategy is to ask teachers how they define that student learning need and how they will measure it. Through continuing discussion, teachers may come to a clearer vision of the learning need. Reminders that they will have to be able to collect data through observation, conversation, and student products can also help refine the student learning need. Another strategy is to ask why? Why do you want students to be engaged? This may help teachers dig deeper and find the actual student learning need. Is this truly a student learning need, or is this more an issue of behavior and classroom management or self-regulation?

Developing Theories of Action

If teachers are struggling with the concept of theories of action, it may be helpful to provide them with alternate definitions:

City et al. (2011) describe a theory of action as

> the story line that makes a vision and a strategy concrete. It gives the leader a line of narrative that leads people through the daily complexity and distractions that compete with the main work. . . . It provides the map that carries the vision through the organization. And it provides a way of testing the assumptions and the suppositions of the vision against the unfolding realities of the work in an actual organization with actual people. (p. 40)

Killion (2008) describes a theory of action as "a comprehensive representation of how the program is intended to work" (p. 41).

Just as the inquiry question may evolve over time, the theories of action may change as new evidence from our work with students challenges our thinking.

Documenting Student Learning

Often the theories of action they have created help teachers determine what to focus on when collecting data (Killion, 2008). For example, in the Lab Class focused on Research Writing, the theories of action were:

- If teachers explicitly teach the research process steps, students will be able to research a topic of interest independently.
- If students have access to a range of technology for their research, they will be engaged in finding and recording information that supports their ideas or is related to their topic.
- If the steps of the research process are "chunked" for students, then students will be able to track their progress to project completion.

When collecting documentation on student learning, teachers need to focus on students' ability to research a topic of interest independently, find and record information related to their topic, and track their project completion progress.

Documenting Teacher Learning

As noted earlier in the chapter, teachers are often not used to documenting their own learning and may be resistant to doing so. Providing time during the meeting for them to record their thoughts is helpful. Some teachers appreciate having templates to scaffold their thinking and can move on from the templates as the Lab Class progresses. Because Lab Class takes place over several months, it is important to document learning throughout the program and not wait until the culminating meeting because teachers may forget their original beliefs and assumptions. It may be helpful to provide prompts for teacher reflection for those teachers who need additional support.

Cognitive Stress

Working on the Inquiry Question, exploring Theories of Action, and completing all the activities in the Launch Meeting is challenging work. Remind teachers that this is an adult learning model—if they need to take a break, they don't need to wait for the facilitator to call one.

Keeping Connected Between Sessions

Technology can be used to keep participants connected and sharing their own learning and their students' learning, whether the Lab Class model involves one school or multiple schools. As a group, participants can consider a range of strategies for using social media and technology for connecting and sharing between Lab Class sessions. Facilitators may be able to set up Discussion Boards within your district's or school's electronic communication system. Other groups may want to have a common hashtag on Twitter to share their own learning as well as that of their students. Be sure to check any district policies on the use of social media before proceeding.

CHAPTER 3

Engaging in Lab Class

> If teachers do use outcome tests and ability scores, and many will be required to do so, they should be aware that every expectation they hold of what a child can and cannot learn should be mistrusted. This means that they should make a hypothesis that they are willing to revise. If we give the learner opportunities and different learning conditions, he might prove the test's predictions to be wrong. Teachers should always be ready to be surprised by any child.
>
> —Clay (1993)

Deprivatizing teacher practice is harder than many people expect (Fullan, 2007). Even in favorable conditions, when implementation strategies are highly supportive, many teachers still prefer private practice (Fullan, Hill, & Crévola, 2006). In Lab Class, we are challenged to find the balance between building a supportive environment that protects the host teachers within a model that provokes teachers to critically examine their practice and requires teachers to open their classrooms to their colleagues and peers.

Since deprivatization is uncomfortable for teachers, specific strategies are used in Lab Class to support teachers including administrative participation in Lab Class, the use of co-created norms, focusing on an inquiry question and theories of action, and descriptive observations of student learning.

Administrative involvement: Lab Class has been structured to provide a supportive environment for teachers to engage in risk taking—trying new instructional practices, challenging current beliefs, and opening their doors to their colleagues. As mentioned in Chapter One, the participation of school administrators can help build an atmosphere of trust. Teachers may struggle at first with new practices, and having the school administrators engaged as co-learners in Lab Class reduces some of that stress.

Review of norms: On the day of a Lab Class classroom observation visit, teachers meet prior to visiting the classroom. After welcoming everyone, the facilitator leads a review of the norms established by the group during the Launch Meeting. These norms also serve as part of the supportive environment for teachers in Lab Class. Revisions can be made to the norms at the beginning or end of any observation session.

Descriptive observations focused on the inquiry question: Before going to the classrooms to observe, the facilitator reviews the inquiry question and reminds teachers to focus their descriptive observations on student conversations, actions, and products that will help us answer our inquiry question. This focused, purposeful observation deters teachers from being distracted by superfluous details and observations that, while interesting, are not relevant to the work. These observations may be set aside for discussion at a later date, if the teachers deem them of sufficient interest. It also keeps the observations focused on student learning and what observers saw or heard, not judgements on what *should* have been happening in the classroom or *why* something was happening. Staying descriptive is another strategy for supporting teachers in deprivatizing their practice.

However, there are times when irrelevant observations may be relevant if teachers dig a bit deeper. An inquiry group was investigating the teaching strategies that would help their students ask higher level questions in Grade 1 and Grade 2 science classes, using Bloom's Taxonomy as a reference. One of the observing teachers recorded an observation about the big, bright windows in the host classroom. At first, this observation seemed unconnected to the inquiry question. But the teacher explained that he thought the windows created opportunities for those students to ask higher level questions about the world outside their classroom, and it became part of a discussion around the impact of classroom conditions and spaces.

Educators have a culture of being kind to one another and of resisting opportunities to critique one another's practice (City et al., 2011). This desire to protect the host during classroom observation visits to encourage deprivatization must be balanced with the need to engage in critical reflection about the nature of teaching practice. Facilitators must "intentionally interrupt" some of our most common practices and beliefs if we want to get deeper with our learning.

Specifically, Katz (2010) lists a number of practices that teachers need to interrupt.

PRACTICES TO INTENTIONALLY INTERRUPT	STRATEGIES USED IN LAB CLASS TO INTENTIONALLY INTERRUPT
The culture of activity and shift to a culture of learning.	• Taking time to explore research and resources before determining next steps. • Documenting student learning and teacher learning.

The cognitive desire to stick to the status quo.	• Exploring research and resources. • Framing our inquiry question around the impact of *teacher practice* on student learning; if we want student learning to change we must examine and change our practice.
The "imposter syndrome" (I have no idea what I'm doing, and I hope no one finds out so I'll keep my practice as private as possible).	• Creating a safe, supportive, collaborative learning community.
The conflation of person and practice where we don't separate who someone is from their professional practice. As a result, it is impossible to discuss someone's practice without it seeming like an attack on the person themself. This leads us to avoid discussing teaching practice.	• Descriptive observations of student learning. • Identification of conditions for student learning. • Asset stance. • Co-created norms that can be adjusted as needed. • Expectation that each teacher serves as host for observations at least once.
The culture of niceness in which productive discussions are nearly impossible because we all want to stay positive and collegial.	• Focus on the impact of our teacher practice on student learning. • Descriptive observations and analysis—focused, professional and nonjudgmental.
Leader as all-knowing expert.	• Facilitator as lead learner, co-learner. • Invitation to school administrators to participate as co-learners.

Katz, (2010).

As a facilitator for Lab Class over many years, I can attest to the enormous impact this model has had on my practice. When I began as an education consultant, my colleagues and I were not planning "sit and get" style workshops. We would carefully plan our professional learning sessions, seeking a balance of pedagogical theory and practical classroom application with opportunities for participants to work independently, in small groups and as a large group. There were opportunities for active engagement with materials and thoughtful reflection. But Lab Class forced us to rethink our role in professional learning from leader to co-learner. Instead of beginning with the pedagogy, we were beginning with what the teachers knew about their students and the teachers' wonderings about their practice. In the past, workshops were held at the district central office so if an additional resource was needed in response to a teacher's question, the consultant could quickly retrieve the resource from the office. In Lab Class, facilitators know the general topic in advance (i.e., communication of thinking in math) but it was not feasible to bring every mathematics resource from the central office. This had an interesting impact on the use of professional resources in Lab Class sessions. First, facilitators began to be more selective about which resources they would bring to the meetings, choosing those that most closely aligned with the teachers' theories of action and inquiry question. Second, teachers began seeking out resources located in their schools—professional books and journals in the principal's office, the school library, and colleagues' classrooms. Books, journals, and resources that had been supplied by central office or by the government that had sat idle on school shelves were now eagerly explored.

Classroom Observations

Pre-Observation Meeting

The day of the Lab Class Observation meeting, all participating teachers meet in a predetermined location—school library, conference room, and so on. The facilitator guides the participants as they review the inquiry question and the co-created norms. If this is a multiple school Lab Class, the facilitator also takes time to thank the host school and administration, point out location of washrooms and host classrooms, and, if necessary, distribute school maps. Host teachers are asked to share a brief introduction to the classroom context to be observed:

- Is this the beginning, middle, or end of the unit?
- Who are the marker students? Why were they chosen?
- Any questions or wonderings he or she is currently considering.

Inquiry question: What is the impact of a focus on spatial relationships on student achievement in all strands of math? (This question was chosen based on research from National Research Council, 2006.)

Example of teacher introduction: I have a Grade 4 class with 25 students; six have identified learning disabilities. We just started our geometry unit yesterday, and I'm curious if our focus on spatial reasoning is going to have an impact on their prior knowledge as we start this unit. I'm expecting them to be able to catch on to this pretty quickly. I have three marker students: Rashid seems to be really strong in number operations but struggles with geometry; Alexis has a reading disability but seems to be doing well in math. How can I use this strength to help her feel better about herself as a learner and be more confident in school? And Amy who is a recent arrival to our school from Germany. She's just learning to speak English and I chose her as a marker student because I'm not sure I have a good understanding of her as a learner.

In our experience, 20 minutes is enough time to collect sufficient classroom observation data for Lab Class. As noted in Chapter Two, students self-selected ahead of time whether they wanted to engage with the observing teachers and could change their minds once the observation began. Observing teachers were asked to enter the classroom as discreetly as possible and engage only as observers for the first 10 minutes, unless a student approached them. Our interactions with students may change their behavior and prevent teachers from getting an accurate observation of their strategies and competencies. During observations, teachers also document learning of students who are not marker students, and those observations are used during the analysis and clustering of observations because they also provide information relevant to the inquiry question.

Teachers can choose to use paper and pen, technology, or whatever means they prefer to record their observations. Teachers have found that participation in Lab Class has helped them develop and refine their documentation of student learning. One teacher wrote in her reflection,

> Documentation needs to be brought back to the children. It should not be posted and forgotten. Documentation must be analyzed if its true value of assessment-for-learning is to be realized. Documentation does not have to be lengthy to communicate what transpired. Be concise and choosy. Things that you want to see come about for children in their learning may not occur or they come about in a different way and that is okay.

Depending on the number of observers and the number of host classrooms, facilitators may want to divide observers into smaller groups and rotate through classrooms so that the number of observers doesn't overwhelm the students in the observed class. In one kindergarten class, a child demonstrated his mathematical skills by loudly counting the "adult visitors"—1, 2, 3 . . . all the way to 11. "There are too many grown-ups in our classroom!" he protested. For subsequent visits, our observation groups were limited to four to five adults per classroom. Rotating through the classrooms will mean that teachers are not all viewing the exact same learning at the exact same time. Since the focus of the Lab Class is not on observing the teacher teach the lesson, this rotation through the classrooms does not have a significant impact on the documentation of student learning in relation to the inquiry question. Careful coordination of the schedule ensures that observations are conducted during the relevant learning time such as mathematics, science, language arts, and so on.

Sample Observation Rotation

TIME	GROUP A (3 TEACHERS)	GROUP B (4 TEACHERS)
9:20–9:40	Classroom One	Classroom Two
9:40–10:00	Classroom Two	Classroom One

Mathematics Block (9:00–10:30 am)

> *When I think out loud I learn more, and the teachers said they learned a lot about how we learn in our class from me. I felt important.*
>
> —*Student*
>
> *It (Lab Class) makes me feel useful because they (the teachers) are using our ideas to make their work better to help us learn. They are taking an interest in us.*
>
> —*Student*

Analysis of Observations

Following the classroom observations, educators return to the meeting area and are invited to select three to five observations from each class that are descriptive, student-focused, asset-based, and related to the inquiry question to share with the group. This is often an aha moment for some teachers because they eliminate observations that were more judgment than description, observations that are focused on materials and not on student learning, observations that are deficit based, and observations that, while interesting, are not related to the inquiry question. Once the teachers select three to five observations per class, each observation is recorded on an individual sticky note, ready for sorting and analysis. Teacher names are not recorded on the sticky notes (adapted from City et al., 2011).

Cluster Observations and Determine Trends

Once everyone has recorded their selected observations on sticky notes, the facilitator invites one teacher to share one of his or her observations. This observation is displayed somewhere in the meeting area such as on a bulletin board, blackboard, or on chart paper, depending on the resources and setup of the meeting area. The facilitator and/or teachers can then determine a category or heading for that

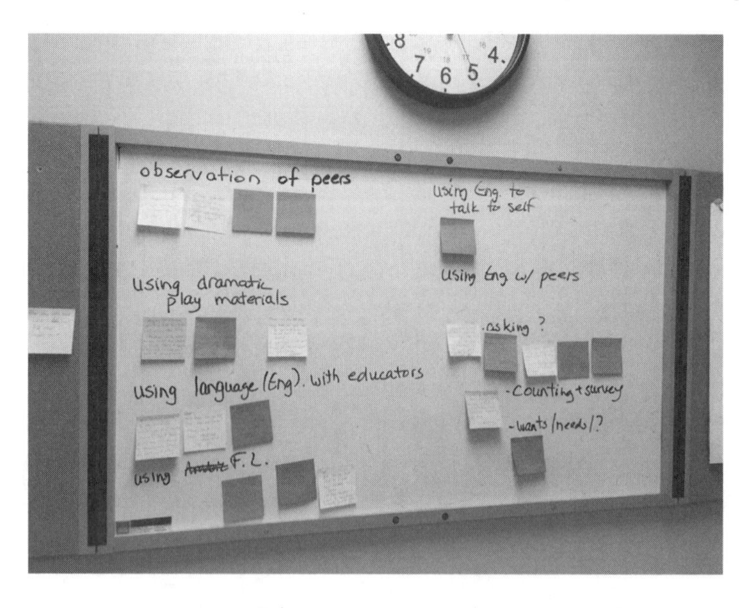

Figure 3.1 Inquiry question: What is the impact of engaging in dramatic play on students' ability to verbally communicate with classmates and educators?

observation. Teachers are then invited to share observations they have recorded that are related to that observation. After all related observations for that category are shared and posted, another teacher can offer an observation and possible category suggestion. Once again, teachers share their observations that may also belong in that category. This continues until all observations are posted and sorted.

It is important to note that these observations can be sorted in different ways, and some observations fit in more than one category. There is not one right way to sort the observations, and teachers may revisit and re-sort the information as our thinking changes. The conversations between colleagues about what the headings might be, where observations might fit, and the connections they see between categories and observations are valuable parts of the professional learning for all participants. These conversations help teachers clarify their thinking and articulate it to others.

Example: Kindergarten to Grade 4

A group of kindergarten to Grade 4 teachers at one school was engaged in a Lab Class focused on student learning in science, social studies, and language. Their inquiry question was: What is the impact of explicitly teaching a variety of oral communication skills and strategies on students' confidence and ability to express their thoughts, ideas, and questions in science and social studies?

(**CCSS.ELA-LITERACY.CCRA.SL.1** Prepare for and participate effectively in a range of conversations and collaborations with diverse partners, building on others' ideas and expressing their own clearly and persuasively.)

Theories of Action

If students are explicitly taught to reflect and think critically about their ideas, thoughts, and questions, then they will see the value of their ideas and have the confidence to share their ideas with others.

If students have multiple and varied opportunities to share their reflections and observations of their learning with others, then they will see themselves as effective communicators.

If students have multiple and varied opportunities to share their reflections and observations of their learning with others, then they will engage more effectively as learners.

What are the indicators for "lack of confidence"?

- Lack of risk taking
- Choosing not to participate
- "I don't know"
- No desire to try new things
- Need for near constant affirmation or feedback from teachers

Clustering Observations From Kindergarten and Grade 2 Classrooms

After observing in two classrooms during their first Lab Class session, the teachers sorted their observations of students communicating their thinking about science and social studies under these headings:

Creating and Articulating a Plan

- Creating a plan for a block house, building, then discussing changes to the plan.
- Student A drawing a very detailed design on blackboard
- Student drew a plan on the chalkboard. She built and then went back to the chalkboard to add before continuing to build.
- This is where the captain sits. (pointing to a space in her block construction)
- After T dismissed to stations, a boy went to plan build and made a house. "I will use big blocks/the big big blocks (tubes) I could use these for skating to help my elbows. I need to use them for my house."

Expressing Their Ideas Orally

- Students were having conversations about topic (e.g., the praying mantis was green, the back legs are . . .)
- "I learned . . . Animals have characteristics." (described characteristics of neighbor)
- At carpet time the student said, "A crocodile is a reptile." Teacher asked how he knew that. "I learned that a reptile is a crocodile!"
- Telling friend "40,000 eggs"—sharing information.
- While making a diagram: "What's that?" "A spike." "Is it poisonous?" "I don't know. Maybe we could check."
- Science vocabulary heard in talk—thorax, abdomen, spider.

Expressing Their Ideas in Writing

- Focused physically on task: eyes on paper, body leaned forward.
- Back and forth between independent—peer help—teacher (particularly in the group of eight).
- Student drew a comic at the bottom of the insect list.
- Student B: "Look, I wrote these all by myself." Adds *killed spider* label. Adds speech bubble, "I need food."
- Strategies I saw—students sounding out words, "sometimes get ideas from web for list."
- Students recording info and ideas on and into lists, webs, and T-charts.

- Three students take their papers to the round table. Look through books in cardboard bin. Return to table with books and laptops and begin to print.
- Organization—book to the side, computer in front, notes at arms' length.
- Student C takes his paper and moves to a spot on his own. Begins printing right away. Teacher, would you like a laptop? No I don't need it. (doesn't look up)
- Student D walks to chart from seat, walks back prints a few letters "slip." Stop. Walks back to chart. Returns to seat. (repeats)
- Student E used the chart for guidance. Referenced it often. Positioned herself to see it.

Expressing Their Ideas Using Technology

- Student F created a video about the praying mantis; play the video, and explain all the parts of a praying mantis and simultaneously told me how he created the video.
- Student G tells another student the parts of a spider and shows several others a video on it on the iPad—watching spider song/video and recording information iPad.
- Using video to research info about spiders, now a music video.
- Students using jigsaw method to add characteristics of animals to lists from a laptop.
- Multiple resources—student looking between book and computer (both with reptile info).
- While Student H had some students' attention with the spider video, he also showed them another "spooky spider" with music to it, and many more students gathered to see it.

Collaboration

- Children vocalizing what they are having trouble with and peers jumping in to help.
- From one student to another: You could do it in pencil. Don't worry, none of us will take it away from you.
- "If you want to you could draw a picture for the teacher to understand better."
- Student J writing and telling Arabic words and songs. "I will teach you."

After reviewing their first sorting attempt, the teachers noticed that many of their observations were related to how students made use of the resources in the classroom including computers, commercial posters, teacher-created charts, nonfiction texts, and writing materials, as well as using the teacher and classmates as resources. In the interest of time, after the meeting two teachers volunteered to re-sort the observations in new headings reflecting student use of resources and share their work electronically with other participants.

Identify Conditions

After the observation sort is completed, the facilitator leads the teachers as they discuss what conditions were present that allowed these trends to emerge. Conditions might include the routines and procedures in place in the classroom, the organization of materials and space in the classroom, or specific teaching strategies. This step of Lab Class provides a context for teachers to reflect on what they are doing and why they are doing it and to share their thinking with their colleagues.

Identifying the conditions can be a challenging step for teachers and facilitators because much of what teachers do in their classrooms has become automatic; they do it without even having to think about it. This can make it difficult for them to articulate what they are doing and why they are doing it. Conscious competence learning theory, also known as Gordon's Ladder or conscious competence matrix, suggests that people go through four stages when learning a new skill, behavior, technique, and so on (Adams, n.d.). The first stage is *unconscious incompetence*—the person doesn't know what they don't know. They are unaware that they have a deficit or may deny the usefulness of the learning. The goal of professional learning is to make the person aware of the potential learning and how it will benefit them. Facilitators want to move them to the second stage of *conscious incompetence*. The person is now aware that they don't know and realizes that they need to learn. This awareness can be brought about in many ways including but not limited to conversations with colleagues, observations of other teachers, professional reading, attending conferences or workshops, a change in teaching assignment, a change in student demographics, or a change in district or school policies. The goal of professional learning at this stage is to provide support as the person develops the skills and abilities. In the third stage, a person is considered *consciously competent*. They can now perform the skill consistently and without assistance, but skill performance still requires concentration and effort. In the fourth stage, *unconsciously competent*, the behavior, skill, or ability has become second nature and the person performs it without even thinking about it. They may have difficulty explaining what they do to another person. Think about how difficult it can be if you are trying to explain to someone all the steps involved in tying your shoes, making a left turn when driving your car, or making your favorite dessert.

When asked to consider what conditions were present that produced the self-reliance observed in students in the kindergarten to Grade 4 Lab Class in the example above (where many students were repeatedly observed independently seeking, retrieving, and then returning the resources they needed for their work), the teachers commented, "We have such a great group of students this year." It seemed that the teachers were unconsciously competent—they did not recognize the steps they had taken to support the students and create the conditions for this behavior. With further prodding from colleagues and the facilitator, the teachers could articulate the classroom procedures and routines that they had taught the students and practiced with them over time that then allowed the students to engage in their work with little teacher support. Their colleagues also pointed out their observations about how the teachers had organized the materials in the room and the impact that had on student independence. The observed teachers shared the various factors they had considered when arranging the room to support independent student work—where to place materials, which materials to put out, and when so that students had enough resources but were not overwhelmed, and how to use the available technology in an efficient and equitable manner. After only a brief discussion, the teachers realized a number of factors that allowed these trends to emerge including consistent classroom routines and procedures, easy student access to a variety of writing materials, clear procedures for use of technology including tablets and laptops, flexible seating arrangements, anchor charts posted at student height in the classroom for student reference, a wide variety of print research materials at different reading levels, research materials organized and displayed in a central location in the classroom, individual student writing folders with personal dictionaries of frequently used words, and procedures for requesting assistance from peers and the teacher.

Through this conversation, the observed teachers moved from unconscious competence to what some are suggesting as a possible fifth step of Gordon's Ladder: Reflective Competence (Taylor, 2007). In Stage Five, teachers reflect on their practice through self-study and peer review, challenging complacency and seeking areas to continue to improve their knowledge and their practice. In reflective competence, teachers may find unconscious errors or new ideas that challenge their thinking, which can then move them back to the earlier stages of conscious incompetence, and the cycle of learning begins again.

The observations made during Lab Class provide us with a good understanding of the Conditions for Learning that are present in the classroom and contribute to the growth observed. Lab Class has empowered our teachers to work together and to share research-based, effective teaching strategies for continued student achievement. Lab Class has also empowered our students to take risks with their learning and to have a voice in how they learn best.

—Principal

Discussing and sharing our observations afterward was very powerful as we categorized the student thinking. We were amazed at what the students were telling us and what they were showing us as learners. We quickly came to the conclusion that we often don't take the time to value the student voice in the classroom. If we commit to listen with intent and purpose to our students, we will surely learn the most about how to better support the children who sit in front of us every day. Their words will guide our actions.

—Vice Principal

While this step of identifying conditions was initially challenging for teachers, and facilitators, it is an opportunity to support and encourage one another and to recognize and celebrate the great learning that was happening by both students and teachers. If the schedule permits, this is an excellent time to take a few minutes to ask teachers to document their own learning as well as the learning of their students. If time was not specifically provided during the meetings for teachers to reflect on and document their own learning, then they often did not take time out of their busy days to do so. Another option is to provide teachers with a template to scaffold them as they document their learning (see Templates E, F, and G).

Following the analysis observations and discussion of trends and conditions, it is also important to take time to thank those teachers whose classrooms were observed in this round of Lab Class. Opening our practice and our learning to colleagues can be uncomfortable; taking a few moments to appreciate their willingness to participate and thank their students for sharing their learning with us is time well spent. Facilitators and/or administrators may want to debrief with the observed teachers privately to determine if any changes should be made to the procedures for the next round of Lab Class.

Revisit the Inquiry Question and Theories of Action

Based on the discussions during the Lab Class meeting, teachers revisit their inquiry question and theories of action. Does this question still reflect their current wonderings? Have their observations and the observations of their colleagues challenged their thinking about their students' strengths and areas of growth? It is not unusual for the inquiry question to evolve after every Lab Class meeting. In the kindergarten to Grade 4 inquiry shared in this chapter, the teachers commented that effective communicators can express their ideas using different modalities including visual arts, drama, and technology. Was their focus on oral language too narrow? Was it not honoring all the ways that students can demonstrate their learning? There was some discussion about changing the scope of the inquiry question to encompass more ways to communicate, but the decision was made to continue the focus on oral language because oral language is the foundation for literacy. Theories of action may also change as our observations and conversations with students challenge our original thinking.

Determine Next Steps: What Does the Research Say?

Using their theories of action as a starting point, teachers determine what professional learning they want to engage in and what resources they might need to support them prior to the next Lab Class meeting (see Template H). These resources could be classroom resources, professional learning resources, or people and/or organizations that could be contacted for additional support. At times, it can be tempting to jump right to what actions teachers want to take in the classroom and what teaching or assessment strategy they want to use to support student learning. This step forces teachers and facilitators to pause and engage in professional research and reading *before* taking action so that actions are based on research and not simply on past practice (Butler & Schnellert, 2012). In this way, we are intentionally interrupting the culture of activity and shifting to a culture of learning (Katz, 2010). Butler and Schnellert (2012) observed that teachers in collaborative professional learning drew on resources such as assessment frameworks and tools, research-informed materials, colleagues, and mentors to inform their practice revisions. In Lab Class, resources that had sat on shelves unused were now opened and investigated as teachers sought more information to deepen their understanding of instructional strategies for supporting their students. Based on the learning needs and the strengths of their students as well as their own professional curiosities, each teacher selects the resource or resources that they wish to explore. As a result, within the Lab Class team, teachers explore different resources that are all linked to the same general inquiry question. This allows the learning to be more precise and meet the needs of teachers and students.

Having choices in resources, and how to access them, enables educators to select what fits best with their preferred modes of learning, the contexts in which they are working, and the time they have available. (Schnellert & Butler, 2014)

One principal commented,

> The observations made during Lab Class provide us with a good understanding of the conditions for learning that are present in the classroom and contribute to the growth observed. Lab Class has empowered our teachers to work together, and to share research-based, effective teaching strategies for continued student achievement.

A teacher noted that

> Lab Class has helped me understand patterns in our students' thinking. When examining their work and conversations, we noticed trends were not the same across divisions and this has led us to examine this further, as this could be a key to a deeper understanding of our students' needs.

Template H

Supports Needed and Next Steps

<table>
<tr><th colspan="2">WHICH IF–THEN STATEMENTS DO YOU WISH TO ENACT?</th></tr>
<tr><td colspan="2">If students have multiple and varied opportunities to share their reflections and observations of their learning with others, then they will see themselves as effective communicators.

(We are noticing that the students are using different modalities to communicate their thinking but still need frequent assurances from teachers—is this OK? They still need to develop more confidence and see themselves as effective communicators.)</td></tr>
<tr><th>WHAT SUPPORTS AND/OR RESOURCES MIGHT YOU NEED?</th><th>WHO MIGHT YOU COLLABORATE WITH?</th></tr>
<tr><td>• Continue to provide different ways for students to share their learning in science, art, technology, writing, and so on.
• Need support with how to assess student achievement of the expectations if they are all doing different things to show their learning.
• How do we communicate with parents so they know that even though one student creates a sculpture of an animal and another child writes a report that they are both still being assessed on the science standards? We may need support sharing this information with students and with parents.
• Information on Core Curriculum Standards for Science.
• Information on creating rubrics.
• More information on supporting students with self-assessment.</td><td>• Assessment consultant from the central office
• School administration
• Same grade colleagues at school</td></tr>
<tr><th colspan="2">CREATE A PLAN FOR THIS WORK:</th></tr>
<tr><td colspan="2">• Review core curriculum standards for science and for language arts. What standards will we be evaluating with this science unit? How can we ensure students are given multiple and varied opportunities to demonstrate their learning?
• Meet with the Assessment and Evaluation Consultant from the district office to learn more about differentiated self-assessment.
• Review literature on self-assessment.
• Create rubric and/or self-assessment checklist with students and post in classroom—if they know the expectations, they can more successfully self-assess. Will they then need less feedback from teachers?</td></tr>
</table>

Proposed Agendas for Lab Class

The agenda or timeline for each Lab Class may vary depending on the number of teachers, the time available, and whether all teachers are from one school or arriving from different schools. The agendas shared below are only examples, and you may modify them to fit the needs of your group. From experience, it is important that the facilitator keep the group moving during the classroom observations so that participants have sufficient time for the remainder of the agenda items.

Multiple Teachers/One School

TIME	AGENDA ITEM
8:30–9:00	Arrival and visit host classrooms prior to students' arrival
9:00–9:20	Meet Review norms Host teachers provide overview; note marker students
9:20–9:40	Observe in first host teacher's room Record observations
9:40–10:00	Observe in second host teacher's classroom Record observations
10:00–10:10	Select observations related to inquiry and record on stickies (Working break: invite teachers to take a break before, during, and after they are done sorting)
10:10–10:45	Cluster Observations and Name Emerging Trends: • Work together to name and cluster emerging trends in the observations shared Identify Conditions Present: • What conditions were present that allowed these trends to emerge—cause for celebration? • Document teacher learning individually
10:45–11:00	Revisit Inquiry Question and Theories of Action
11:00–11:15	Consider Next Steps: What are some ideas for the next level of work based on what was uncovered through observing students? Choose date, time, and location of host classrooms for next Lab Class
11:15–11:45	Professional Learning—reading, research

Proposed Agenda: Half-Day Meeting

<table>
<tr><th>TIME</th><th colspan="2">AGENDA ITEM</th></tr>
<tr><td>8:30–9:00</td><td colspan="2">Arrival and visit host classrooms prior to students' arrival</td></tr>
<tr><td>9:00–9:20</td><td colspan="2">Meet
Review norms
Host teachers provide overview; note marker students</td></tr>
<tr><td>9:20–9:40</td><td>Group A: Observe in Classroom One</td><td>Group B: Observe in Classroom Two</td></tr>
<tr><td>9:40–10:00</td><td>Group B: Observe in Classroom One</td><td>Group A: Observe in Classroom Two</td></tr>
<tr><td>10:00–10:10</td><td colspan="2">Select observations related to inquiry and record on stickies
(Working break: invite teachers to take a break before, during, and after they are done sorting)</td></tr>
<tr><td>10:10–10:45</td><td colspan="2">Cluster Observations and Name Emerging Trends:
• Work together to name and cluster emerging trends in the observations shared
Identify Conditions Present:
• What conditions were present that allowed these trends to emerge—cause for celebration?
• Document teacher learning individually</td></tr>
<tr><td>10:45–11:00</td><td colspan="2">Revisit Inquiry Question and Theories of Action</td></tr>
<tr><td>11:00–11:15</td><td colspan="2">Consider Next Steps:
What are some ideas for the next level of work based on what was uncovered through observing students?
Choose date, time, and location of host classrooms for next Lab Class</td></tr>
<tr><td>11:15–11:45</td><td colspan="2">Professional Learning—reading, research</td></tr>
</table>

Proposed Agenda: Half-Day Meeting With Observation Rotations

Multiple Teachers/Multiple Schools

TIME	AGENDA ITEM
9:00–9:20	Meet Review norms Host teacher provides overview; note marker students

TIME	AGENDA ITEM
9:20–9:40	Observe student learning in host teacher's room Record observations
9:40–9:45	Return to meeting area Select observations related to inquiry and record on stickies
9:45–10:05	Cluster Observations and Name Emerging Trends: • Work together to name and cluster emerging trends in the observations shared Identify Conditions Present: • What conditions were present that allowed these trends to emerge—cause for celebration? • Document teacher learning individually
10:05–10:10	Revisit Inquiry Question and Theories of Action
10:10–10:40	Consider Next Steps: What are some ideas for the next level of work based on what was uncovered through observing students? Professional Learning—reading, research Choose date, time, and location of host classrooms for next Lab Class

Proposed Agenda: 100-Minute PLC Meeting

TIME	AGENDA ITEM
8:30–9:00	Arrival and visit host classroom prior to students' arrival
9:00–9:10	Meet Review norms Host teacher provides overview; note marker students
9:10–9:30	Observe in host teacher's room Record observations
9:30–10:00	View videos from other participating teachers of their marker students Record observations

(Continued)

(Continued)

TIME	AGENDA ITEM
10:00–10:10	Select observations related to inquiry and record on stickies (Working break: invite teachers to take a break before, during, and after they are done sorting)
10:10–10:45	Cluster Observations and Name Emerging Trends: • Work together to name and cluster emerging trends in the observations shared Identify Conditions Present: • What conditions were present that allowed these trends to emerge—cause for celebration? • Document teacher learning individually
10:45–11:00	Revisit Inquiry Question and Theories of Action
11:00–11:15	Consider Next Steps: What are some ideas for the next level of work based on what was uncovered through observing students? Choose date, time, and location of host classrooms for next Lab Class
11:15–11:45	Professional Learning—reading, research

Proposed Agenda: Half-Day Lab Class

Available for download at **resources.corwin.com/LabClass**

Troubleshooting Tips

Absent marker students: Several times when we arrived at a school for Lab Class one or more of the marker students were absent. In that case, we simply asked the teachers to choose other students for us to observe during our observation time, preferably students with similar learning strengths and needs to the absent student.

Classroom observation: One teacher who participated in Lab Class informed us at the Launch Meeting that she had a student with special needs in her class who might find it distressing to have classroom visitors. During our first visit to her classroom, she said that he was having a difficult day and having visitors to the classroom would not be possible. Instead, we made our observations from videos of her marker students that she had taken earlier that week. On our second observation visit, a few months later, the education assistant aligned to the class took the student to the computer lab while the observing teachers were in the classroom.

Difficulty remaining descriptive: Some teachers struggle initially to remain descriptive in their observations of students. Allowing them to sort their observations and choose three to five observations that are asset based, descriptive and related to the inquiry often eliminates the more inferential observations. If not, when those observations are shared the facilitator can ask prompting questions such as "How do you know?" and "What makes you think that?" This can help uncover the evidence that lead to inferences such as "the students were engaged in the lesson" or "the student enjoyed the activity."

Identifying conditions: It is important for facilitators to put aside their preconceived notions of what they think the teachers will identify as the conditions that allowed the observed trends to emerge and accept those offered by the participants. There may be disagreement between participants about the conditions, but the discussion that arises during these disagreements can help expose new or revised theories of action or areas for further professional learning.

CHAPTER 4

Consolidation and Culmination of Lab Class

> We are inclined to think of reflection as something quiet and personal. My argument here is that reflection is action-oriented, social and political. Its "product" is praxis (informed, committed action), the most eloquent and socially significant form of human action.
>
> —Kemmis (1985)

After all the observation visits have been held, Lab Class concludes with a final culminating networked learning session. At this meeting the facilitator guides the participants through a reflection on their learning, the students' learning, and their team's collaborative learning journey using Lab Class. At this meeting, participants also determine who they want to share their learning with and how they want to share their learning. If schools are using professional learning community (PLC) time for Lab Class, this Consolidation Meeting may take place over two or more sessions. The Consolidation Meeting is also a time to have participants reflect on the Lab Class process and provide feedback for the facilitators on what worked and what they feel could be improved in this learning model.

Reflect on the Learning

The meeting begins with an opportunity for each teacher to individually and independently reflect on their own learning and the learning demonstrated by the students in their own class. Facilitators may wish to use Templates E, F, or G (see pages 131–133) as a prompt for written teacher reflection or use some of the prompting questions from these templates as a guide. After each teacher has completed their written reflection, facilitators provide a large block of time for sharing. First, each teacher shares their professional learning while one teacher from the group acts as the recorder. Once all teachers have shared their learning, the recorder notes the commonalities shared by the teachers. Depending on the template and prompting questions selected by the facilitator, the teachers continue sharing, recording, and noting commonalities. In networks with more than one school, this sharing takes place in school teams.

Next, the facilitator guides the school teams in returning to the inquiry question and the theories of action: Was the question answered? Did our theories of action reflect the actions we took as educators and the learning experienced by the students? Did we achieve the results we expected? Why or why not? What have we learned? What have our students learned? What were the pivotal moments on our journey? Facilitators may wish to appoint one person as the recorder for the group to record the discussions, or the role may be shared with a different recorder for each question so that everyone has an opportunity to participate in the discussion. Template G can be used to record information, or teams may choose another format.

Lab Class has helped open our doors to visit other classrooms and divisions in our school. It has reminded me to think about what learning the students have done and has provided me with data about what my students can do! It has supported my learning about documentation, inquiry, and assessment.

—Teacher

Lab Class has been a great way for teachers and administration to learn from our students. When listening to student conversations and observing their choices of strategies in mathematics problem solving, we have gained a new perspective on what is "really going on" with student thinking. Since Lab Class is an asset-based model focused on student learning, it is a nonjudgmental process. It is a safe way for teachers to learn about their students. The student voice is greatly valued in this process, and students are proud of the fact that we are learning new things from them. One of the most positive things about Lab Class is the fact that teachers see evidence of their hard work in the trends of the observed data, and as a group, we can often come up with a collective solution of how to better target instruction to improve student achievement.

—Principal

Template G

Teacher Reflection—Sample Three

SCHOOL:		
INQUIRY QUESTION:		
What is the impact of explicitly teaching oral language (metacognition skills) on students' confidence and ability to express their thoughts, ideas, and questions within an inquiry-based environment?		
THEORIES OF ACTION:		
If students are explicitly taught to reflect and think critically about their ideas, thoughts, and questions, then they will see the value of their ideas and have the confidence to share their ideas with others. • If teachers provide students with multiple and varied opportunities to share their reflections and observations of their learning with others, then they will see themselves as effective communicators. • If teachers provide students with multiple and varied opportunities to share their reflections and observations of their learning with others, then they will engage more effectively as learners.		
INCLUDE EVIDENCE RELATED TO THE GUIDING QUESTIONS	**STUDENT LEARNING**	**EDUCATOR LEARNING**
(Include artifacts and student and educator quotes) • What have you learned? • What were pivotal moments for teachers and students? • What evidence did you collect to address your inquiry question and theory of action statements? • Why that evidence? • What patterns or items of interest did you notice? • Limitations or challenges?	• Students have learned that they learn from asking questions and asking questions helps them with their learning. • Students see value in their sharing. • Students seem more willing to share when they feel that someone will be learning from their experience. • Students are able to listen with a purpose. • Kindergarten student quote: "You're here with the other teachers? (yes) Excuse me, I need to go share with them." Evidence: Student work, photos of student work and collaboration, Post-It notes with teacher observations of student learning sorted by categories, anecdotal notes, student oral language logs, photos of student work, samples of student talk, photos of documentation panels	What we have learned and Pivotal Moments for Educators: • Aha! moments when students notice something and have the ability to describe and explain. Their pride as well as their confidence is noticeable. • We were doing "Let's Talk About It" as a whole group lesson, and students were just copying their classmates. Now, it is their idea and reflection. • We found that when we helped students think about how they learned best, we could provide tiered instruction with opportunities for independent research, "sit and get," and reading books. • Students needed support to ask questions and take responsibility or ownership of the learning. • Students needed explicit teaching of the inquiry process. We engaged in the four steps of inquiry, and students learned that their ideas could be explored and further questioned.

(Continued)

(Continued)

INCLUDE EVIDENCE RELATED TO THE GUIDING QUESTIONS	STUDENT LEARNING	EDUCATOR LEARNING
	Collecting this evidence helped us focus on the students and their learning, as well as our own professional learning. Patterns and Items of Interest: • Noticed that some students needed explicit teaching about inquiry. • From sharing sessions, the kindergarten educators noticed a change in the questions that students asked. • Sharing their learning had an interesting impact: Students were motivated to share their knowledge because they knew that they had an attentive audience; students focused on how to organize their work so others could understand; they really understood that speaking, writing, and presenting their ideas was for the purpose to communicate a message. • We realized that we couldn't assume that students had the vocabulary to express their ideas, and educators used that moment to use prompts and encouragement to help students find their words. Limitations and Challenges: We found that as time progressed our sorting of the student observation data changed as our comfort level with inquiry grew and our focus shifted from inquiry to a broader scope.	Evidence: Post-It notes of teacher observations of student learning sorted by categories, photos of student work, and photos of documentation panels with educator annotation. We also created an Evernote page, which tracked our project chronologically with notes and photos. Patterns and Items of Interest: • We had to determine what level of scaffolding was necessary for each student to engage in the inquiry process successfully. • Stages of inquiry needed to be explicitly taught and displayed in the classroom. • Students were given a range of opportunities to share their learning. Limitations and Challenges: Some educators wondered what it would look like to have a control group for comparison as part of our inquiry.

• What are the implications of student learning on change in teacher practice? • What have you learned as a collaborative team about working and learning together? • What are the implications for further actions or further questions?	Implications of Student Learning on Educator Practice: • We have to be fluid and go with the flow of our students and be more receptive to what the needs and strengths of the students are and where they are at. • Modeling that it is okay not to know the answer to a question, and even as adults, we might need to figure that out or that students could figure it out to help us teach something new. • Be open to different ways to learn about the same topic. • You don't have to indulge every single student interest. Learn the difference between a fleeting interest and something that the students are passionately interested in. • Proven effective educator practices will create positive change, but this constantly evolves because you don't know what strategy will work until you try. So you have to try different things and then evaluate them on their merits and your instincts. What we have learned about working and learning together as a collaborative team: • The steps, the progress, the process, and the growth of the journey that goes with working with partners are the most positive, not just the product at the end. • We are accepting of the fact that we are all trying at our own pace. • We have to be doing just as much learning as the students. • Questioning our own practices along the way is important for growth. • We feel more secure knowing that it all doesn't end when the year is done. In the following grade, some of the same inquiry practices will continue and be built on. Implications for further actions or further questions: • It is important to embrace all different kinds of learners; how do we make sure that no children are left behind? • How do we develop better provocations that will hook the students on multiple levels leading to cross-curricular implications? • How can we use guiding questions to help guide the inquiry? Using framing questions to review student inquiry—how is knowing this going to help your learning? Is that helping us answer our question?

If the Lab Class involved multiple schools with multiple teachers with separate inquiry questions and theories of action for each school, then facilitators may wish to have each school share a summary of their discussion with the large group. If time permits, the participants can look for commonalities in the learning between the schools as well as explore what learning was unique to each school.

Develop a Communication Plan

Once the team has summarized their professional learning and their students' learning from this Lab Class experience, they need to decide who they want to share their learning with and how they want to share their learning. Potential audiences could include:

- Teachers, colleagues at their school, at other schools in their district, or beyond their district
- Administrators and superintendents
- Students
- Parents and the community
- Trustees and school board officials
- Other audiences

Initially student and teacher learning from Lab Class was documented by the facilitators with formal written reports (see Templates I and J). These reports were submitted to the participating schools as well as the Ministry of Education, which had provided funding. However, these reports were rather formal and not very reader-friendly so they had little reach beyond the Lab Class participants. Giving participants the ownership of communicating their learning leads to a wide variety of strategies and formats for sharing with a range of audiences.

Bulletin board panels were used to document and share student learning. The intended audiences for this communication were colleagues at the school and parents. The teachers hoped that the documentation of student learning and captions describing the learning process would encourage interested colleagues to ask questions and try new teaching strategies in their classrooms. This sharing was not only a culminating activity but also was ongoing throughout the Lab Class process. Photos of the bulletin board documentation were shared on social media for parents who did not usually visit the school. One teacher noted, "Our purposeful documentation has provided parents with an opportunity to make meaning of their child's learning."

Social media: One multiple school group used Twitter to share their learning and created a hashtag that they shared with colleagues, their administrators, and parents so everyone could follow the student and teacher learning. This Twitter hashtag allowed them to continue sharing once the formal Lab Class period had ended. Teachers and facilitators should check their district's policies regarding the use of social media if they wish to use this strategy.

Learning Buddies: At one school, staff members who were participating in Lab Class realized that several colleagues were asking questions and seemed interested in learning more about the changes the teachers were making in their math instruction and the impact it was having on student learning. They proposed that each teacher who had participated in Lab Class would offer to act as a "learning buddy'" with another interested teacher who had not participated. They would share their inquiry questions, their learning, their resources, and their lesson plans with their partner.

Figure 4.1 K1 Math Infographic

If a student is able to discuss school mathematics with family and friends, just as one would discuss a favorite book or good movie, then that student has experienced meaningful math learning and teaching. (Gadanidis & Hughes, 2011, p. 487)

We wondered . . .

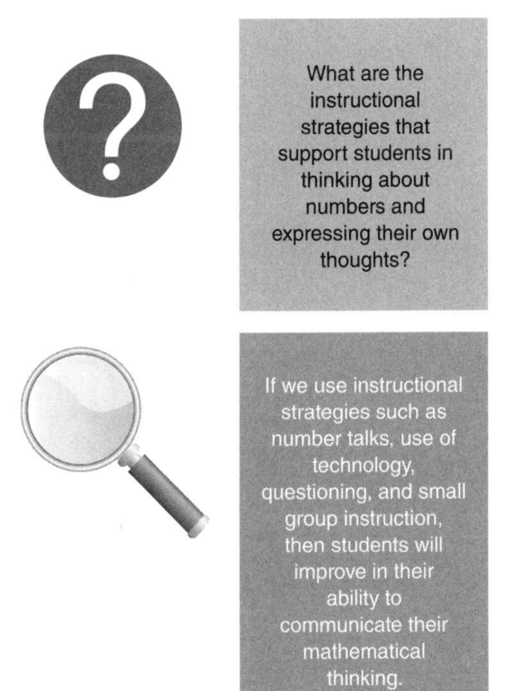

Children's thinking is not limited to the concrete and mechanical; they are capable of complex and abstract mathematics.

Oral, written, and physical communication make mathematics observable. Through communication, students reflect on, clarify, and expand their ideas and understanding of mathematical relationships.

Through listening, talking, and writing about mathematics, students are prompted to organize, re-organize, and consolidate their thinking and understanding.

(Continued)

(Continued)

We tried . . .

Photo by Elizabeth Jenks

Concrete manipulatives provide students with tactical experiences to help them model, describe, and explore mathematics.

Manipulatives

Some math apps are games with little opportunity for students to develop problem-solving skills. It is important to focus on apps that students can use as tools for thinking and communication.

Technology

Young children may have a beginning understanding of math concepts but often they lack the language to communicate their ideas about them.

Questioning and Prompting

Students who have developed the ability to calculate mentally can select from and use a variety of procedures that take advantage of their knowledge and understanding of numbers, the operations, and their properties.

Mental Math

Educators need to ask open-ended questions and engage in conversations that provide students opportunities to take the lead. Interactions of this nature are best suited to small group situations.

Small Group Instruction

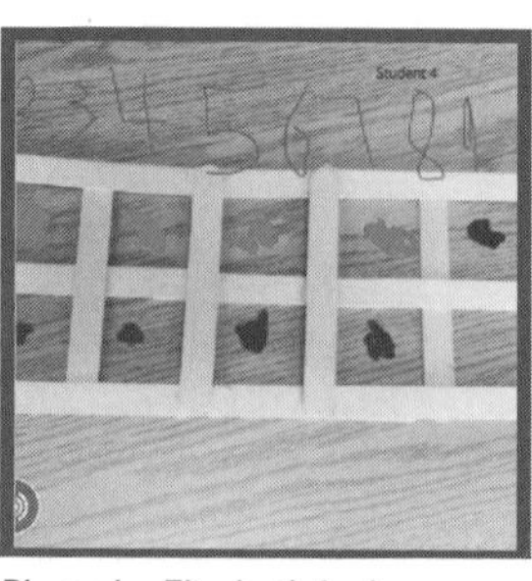
Photo by Elizabeth Jenks

We noticed . . .

- Marker students used math vocabulary when speaking.
- Their vocabulary transferred to other areas of math (e.g., number talks strategies were used by the students when communicating and thinking in other areas of math).
- Marker students were able to notice and explain what they were doing (e.g., Instead of saying "I don't know," they could identify strategies and the kinds of math they were engaged in).
- Many students seemed to be more confident. Because they knew strategies, they would name them. They seemed more confident when speaking with the teacher, and their answers were more detailed. The students had lots more to say about math.
- The students named and used a wide range of manipulatives.

Young children are capable of dealing with a comprehensive and challenging mathematics curriculum and with genuinely interesting mathematics ideas. They engage readily in math through play and informal learning.

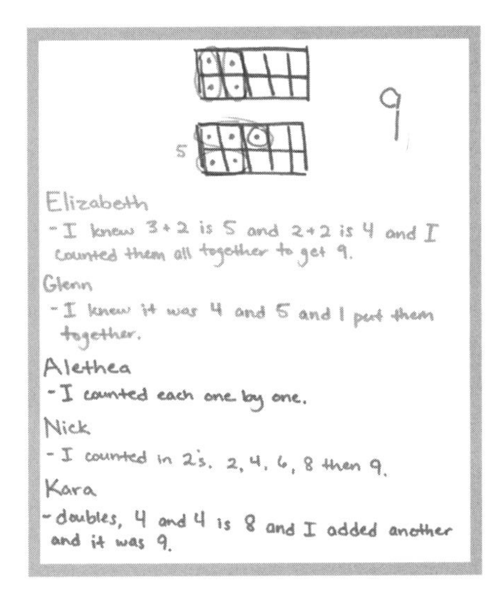

Infographics, Flyers, and Brochures: Teachers have created infographics, flyers, and brochures to share their learning with a wide range of audiences including colleagues, parents, administrators, and teachers in other districts. We have also shared these documents at local and regional learning fairs.

Learning Fair: At the end of the year, we offered a district learning fair and invited teams that had been participating in a variety of different professional learning models to come and share their learning with their colleagues. Trustees and administrators were also invited. Educators and administrators could learn more about the student and teacher learning as well as about the different professional learning models. A brief one page summary of Lab Class was available for participants.

Lab Class: Getting Started

Preparing for Lab Class

Step 1. Determine a Focus for Collaborative Work.

a. Triangulate Data:

i. Student Capabilities

ii. Student Areas for Growth

iii. Professional Curiosities

b. Develop your team's question:

i. See handout for ideas

c. Defining Lab Class:

i. This is a professional learning structure that is focused on student conversation, action, and product in an effort to improve student learning.

ii. This involves taking descriptive observations of student conversation, action, and product in each other's classrooms.

iii. This is an asset-oriented approach; all involved are careful to ensure our work is framed in the positive.

Step 2. Learn to Be Descriptive.

a. Why be descriptive:

i. Read and discuss the excerpts from "Instructional Round."

b. How to be descriptive:

i. Engage in the Photo Activity where partners aim to be descriptive while describing photos to each other.

c. Practice taking descriptive observations:

i. Watch the online clip and record your observations related to the identified student learning need.

ii. Analyze your observation notes to ensure they are descriptive and relate to the focus.

iii. Begin to cluster and describe trends evolving from the observations taken from this clip.

Engaging in Lab Class

Step 3. Discuss Norms.

a. Work together to determine norms that would be appropriate for this practice. For example:

i. be positive; focus on competencies;

ii. record observations of student conversation, action, and product; and

iii. silently observe for at least 10 minutes before asking any questions.

b. Ensure any questions asked are open ended

c. Minimize hallway conversations

Step 4. Visit classrooms to take descriptive observations of **student conversation, action, and product.**

a. 20 min. in each classroom has proven to be enough time for observations.

Step 5. Analyze Individual Observations.

a. Participants select three to five observations that are descriptive, student focused, asset based, and related to the identified student learning focus to share with the group.

Step 6. Cluster Observations and Name Emerging Trends.

a. Work together to name and cluster emerging trends in the observations shared.

Step 7. Identify Conditions Present.

a. What conditions were present that allowed these trends to emerge—cause for celebration?

Step 8. Determine Next Steps.

a. What are some ideas for the next level of work based on what was uncovered through Lab Class?

i. Engage in professional learning related to these next steps and then engage in Lab Class again to determine impact.

Consolidation and Culmination

Step 9. Share the Learning.

a. Reflect on your team's collaborative inquiry journey.

b. Determine with whom you want to share your learning and how you might share it.

c. Enact your communication plan.

Presentations: Because teachers are collecting documentation of student learning as well as professional learning, there is usually ample material to choose from to put together a presentation that can then be shared with a variety of audiences including parents, administrators, and board officials.

Here is a format we have used for PowerPoint presentations about our Lab Class learning:

- *Slide One:* Overview of participating schools
- *Slide Two:* Inquiry question
- *Slide Three:* Theories of action
- *Slides Four through Eight (or more):* Examples of student learning and teacher learning
- *Final slide:* Next steps

Publications: Just as the plentiful documentation can be used to create a presentation, it can also be used to write an article for publication in local or national teachers' journals and magazines. Teachers and facilitators should check with their district for policies regarding publication.

Book Talks: As each teacher was exploring different resources—books, articles, websites, journals, and so on—we often found certain resources that were relevant for the whole group and pivotal to the learning journey. Teachers organized book talks to share these resources with interested colleagues and administrators.

In large teams, teachers may choose to break into smaller teams to work on different communication strategies based on their own interests, strengths, and preferences. Some teachers may be more comfortable preparing and delivering a presentation to audiences while others might prefer to create a brochure or blog.

Ensure that the team has a clear communication plan in place and that each person knows his or her role in the plan. The communication plan should have specific timelines, and the group may choose one person to act as the plan manager to follow up with participants to confirm the communication plan is enacted. If time permits, invite each group of teachers to share their communication strategy with the whole group for feedback.

Last, we want to give participants an opportunity to provide feedback on the Lab Class model to guide our work as facilitators. Depending on the time, this can be done quickly by distributing a feedback sheet such as Templates K and L (see pages 137 and 138), or groups may create their own format. Templates K and L can also be sent out online using a website such as SurveyMonkey, and teachers could complete independently; however, we have found that the percentage of teachers completing and submitting the feedback forms increases significantly when time is provided during the Consolidation Meeting.

If time permits, instead of individual feedback, facilitators could have each team complete feedback as a group using the templates or a protocol such as World Café or Chalk Talk. The questions in the samples provided here can be adapted so that they reflect the goals of the facilitators and the schools that were participating in Lab Class.

World Café Protocol

Step 1. Groups of four to six teachers sit together at each table. Each table group selects a leader.

Step 2. The leader's role is to record the major points of the conversation and then, later, to summarize the conversation. A large sheet of chart paper and a marker is used to record the points so that all participants can easily see what is being recorded.

Step 3. The facilitator posts the first question and informs the groups how much time they have to discuss this question.

Step 4. The group discusses the question while the leader records key points.

Step 5. Time is called. The leader stays at the table; the rest of the group moves to another table. They can move as a whole group, or if there are many tables, they can disperse and create new groups.

Step 6. The leader, who had remained at the table, presents a summary of the conversation recorded from the previous group to the new group.

Step 7. Each table selects a new leader. The new leader takes a fresh sheet of chart paper.

Step 8. The facilitator provides the groups with the next prompting question and the time limit. The table leader records major points of the conversation and then, later, summarizes the conversation.

Step 9. The group discusses the topic until time is called.

Step 10. Repeat the process until all questions have been discussed—usually three to five questions.

Step 11. After the final round, the last group of leaders presents to the whole group.

Adapted from Gueswel (2011).

Chalk Talk

Chalk Talk is a silent way for teachers (and students) to reflect on learning.

Materials: chalk and chalkboard, or paper posted on the wall and markers, or white board and dry erase markers

1. Facilitator briefly explains that Chalk Talk is a silent activity. No one may talk but anyone may add to the chalk talk.
2. The facilitator writes the prompting questions at different areas of the paper/chalkboard/white board. Be sure to spread the questions around the room so that participants have space to read, write, and move about.
3. Each participant takes a piece of chalk or marker. People write where and when they wish; they may comment on one question or them all. Allow lots of wait time.
4. The facilitator can model (silently) how to interact with the comments posted by
   a. writing questions about a comment,
   b. adding his or her own comments,
   c. connecting two comments together with a line, or
   d. adding a question mark next to a comment where they would like more information.

Adapted from Wentforth for the NSRF, (2014). Originally developed by Smith for Foxfire Fund, (2009).

Possible prompting questions for World Café and Chalk Talk

- How has participating in Lab Class impacted your teaching practice?
- How has participating in Lab Class impacted your documentation of student learning?
- If you could change one thing about Lab Class, what would you change and why?
- What was the impact of having other teachers observe your students and your class?

Template K

Lab Class Feedback—Exit Ticket

Date:

WHAT I CAME EXPECTING ...	WHAT I GOT ...
I APPRECIATED ...	**WHAT I STILL NEED ...**

Template L

Lab Class Feedback—Survey

Please consider the impact that each of the Lab Class components has had on your professional learning.

1—no impact

2—little impact

3—moderate impact

4—strong impact

Developing (and revising) an Inquiry Question:	1	2	3	4
Developing (and revising) Theories of Action:	1	2	3	4
Collecting Evidence of Learning with Marker Students:	1	2	3	4
Observing Students in Other Classes:	1	2	3	4
Teachers Observing My Students:	1	2	3	4
Collaboratively Sorting Lab Class Observations and Identifying Conditions:	1	2	3	4
Professional Reading and Exploring Research:	1	2	3	4
Reflecting and Documenting My Professional Learning:	1	2	3	4

Comments:

Proposed Agendas for the Consolidation Meeting

The agenda or timeline for the Consolidation Meeting may vary depending on the number of teachers, the time available, and whether all teachers are from one school or arriving from different schools. The agendas shared below are only examples, and you may modify them to fit the needs of your group.

Multiple Teachers/One School

TIME	AGENDA ITEM
9:00–9:50	Meet Review inquiry question and theories of action • Was the question answered? • Did our theories of action reflect the actions we took as educators and the learning experienced by the students? • Did we achieve the results we expected? • Why or why not? What have we learned? • What have our students learned? • What were the pivotal moments on our journey?
9:50–10:20	Develop a communication plan • Who is our audience(s)? • How will we reach them? • Begin to draft communication documents—e-mail, invitations, presentations, brochures, posters, and so on.
10:20–10:30	Consider next steps: Review the communication plan: What are the next steps? Establish specific responsibilities for participants with timelines. Who will follow up to ensure the communication plan continues to move forward? Professional Learning: After reviewing the inquiry question and theories of action, is there further reading and research to explore?
10:30–10:40	Exit Ticket: Feedback on Lab Class model completed individually

Proposed Agenda: 100-Minute PLC Consolidation Meeting

TIME	AGENDA ITEM
9:00–9:50	Meet Review inquiry question and theories of action • Was the question answered? • Did our theories of action reflect the actions we took as educators and the learning experienced by the students? • Did we achieve the results we expected? • Why or why not? What have we learned? • What have our students learned? • What were the pivotal moments on our journey?
9:50–10:10	Develop a communication plan • Who is our audience(s)? • How will we reach them? • If the group wishes, they may break into smaller groups to implement more than one communication strategy.
10:10–11:00	Implement communication plan • Review the communication plan—what are the next steps? • Facilitator ensures each participant is clear on their role in the plan • Begin to draft communication documents—e-mail, invitations, presentations, brochures, posters, and so on.
11:00–11:30	If the participants have created smaller groups, this time can be used for each group to share their progress and plans. If not, use this time to gather feedback on Lab Class model.
11:30–11:45	Establish specific responsibilities for participants with timelines. Who will follow up to ensure the communication plan continues to move forward? Professional Learning: After reviewing the inquiry question and theories of action is there further reading and research to explore? Thank all participants!

Proposed Agenda: Half-Day Consolidation Meeting

Multiple Teachers/Multiple Schools

TIME	AGENDA ITEM
9:00–9:50	Meet Review inquiry question and theories of action (participants work with teams from their own school) • Was the question answered? • Did our theories of action reflect the actions we took as educators and the learning experienced by the students? • Did we achieve the results we expected? • Why or why not? What have we learned? • What have our students learned? • What were the pivotal moments on our journey?
9:50–10:10	Develop a communication plan (participants work with teams from their own school) • Who is our audience(s)? • How will we reach them? • If the group wishes, they may break into smaller groups to implement more than one communication strategy.
10:10–11:00	Implement communication plan (participants work with teams from their own school) • Review the communication plan; what are the next steps? • Facilitator ensures each participant is clear on their role in the plan. • Begin to draft communication documents—e-mail, invitations, presentations, brochures, posters, and so on.
11:00–11:20	Each school shares their communication plan with the large group.
11:20–11:35	Establish specific responsibilities for participants with timelines. Who will follow up to ensure the communication plan continues to move forward? Professional learning: After reviewing the inquiry question and theories of action is there further reading and research to explore?
11:30–11:45	Gather feedback on Lab Class Model Thank all participants!

Proposed Agenda: Half-Day Consolidation Meeting

<table>
<tr><th>TIME</th><th>AGENDA ITEM</th></tr>
<tr><td>9:00–9:50</td><td>Meet

Review inquiry question and theories of action (participants work with teams from their own school)

• Was the question answered?
• Did our theories of action reflect the actions we took as educators and the learning experienced by the students?
• Did we achieve the results we expected?
• Why or why not? What have we learned?
• What have our students learned?
• What were the pivotal moments on our journey?</td></tr>
<tr><td>9:50–10:15</td><td>Each school shares the results of their discussion above

Time for Q & A</td></tr>
<tr><td>10:15–10:45</td><td>Develop a communication plan (participants work with teams from their own school)

• Who is our audience(s)?
• How will we reach them?
• If the group wishes, the groups may break into smaller groups to implement more than one communication strategy.</td></tr>
<tr><td>10:45–11:45</td><td>Implement communication plan (participants work with teams from their own school)

• Review the communication plan; what are the next steps?
• Facilitator ensures each participant is clear on their role in the plan
• Begin to draft communication documents—e-mail, invitations, presentations, brochures, posters, and so on.</td></tr>
<tr><td>11:45–12:30</td><td>Lunch</td></tr>
<tr><td>12:30–1:10</td><td>Each group shares their communication plan with the large group.</td></tr>
<tr><td>1:10–1:30</td><td>Establish specific responsibilities for participants with timelines. Who will follow up to ensure the communication plan continues to move forward?</td></tr>
<tr><td>1:30–2:00</td><td>Professional Learning: After reviewing the inquiry question and theories of action, is there further reading and research to explore?</td></tr>
<tr><td>2:00–2:15</td><td>Break</td></tr>
<tr><td>2:15–2:45</td><td>Gather feedback on Lab Class model using World Café protocol.</td></tr>
<tr><td>2:45–3:00</td><td>Thank all participants.

Dismissal</td></tr>
</table>

Proposed Agenda: Full-Day Consolidation Meeting

Available for download at **resources.corwin.com/LabClass**

Lab Class Examples

> When schools and school districts offer situated, sustained, collaborative, inquiry-oriented professional development, they enable educators to effectively bridge theory and practice and personalize their learning.
>
> —Schnellert & Butler (2016)

This chapter presents one example of a Lab Class for each of the three possible models: multiple teachers/one school, multiple teachers/multiple schools, and one teacher/multiple schools. Each summary was created at the culmination of the Lab Class journey, and each is written in a different style as our learning evolved. All school names have been changed to ensure anonymity.

Lab Class One: Multiple Teachers/One School

Co-investigators:

- Teacher Consultant: Kindergarten and Primary
- 11 Elementary Teachers: Kindergarten and Grade 1 classrooms
- Principal and Vice Principal

ABC Public School is a French Immersion school with a student population of approximately 600 students located in an urban area. It has a very diverse student population with a large number of English as a Second Language students and parents. The administration at the school is very interested in using collaborative inquiry as a model for moving more play-based learning from kindergarten to Grade 1 classrooms.

Inquiry Question

What is the impact of integrating the Arts on student achievement in reading, specifically on: making connections, making inferences, expressing personal thoughts and feelings about what has been read, and identifying the point of view of the speaker in a piece of text and suggesting a possible alternative perspective. (Teachers could differentiate by selecting specific art strands—visual arts, drama, dance, or music—based on student need and interest. Teachers could choose to focus on reading skills depending on the strengths and needs of their students.)

Common Core Standards

Key Ideas and Details:

CCSS.ELA-LITERACY.CCRA.R.1 Read closely to determine what the text says explicitly and to make logical inferences from it; cite specific textual evidence when writing or speaking to support conclusions drawn from the text.

CCSS.ELA-LITERACY.CCRA.R.6 Assess how point of view or purpose shapes the content and style of a text.

CCSS.ELA-LITERACY.CCRA.R.9 Analyze how two or more texts address similar themes or topics in order to build knowledge or to compare the approaches the authors take.

The Inquiry Focus

Integrating language arts and the arts. Each year the district conducts a review of their programs to ensure that our classroom practice matches our theory of action (Argyris, 1995). The data from the previous year's review indicates that teachers need additional support around shared reading and guided reading, as well as in the implementation of the arts curriculum. Our research review is still in the initial stages, and we may expand our review once we determine the strands of the arts that students and teachers are interested in exploring in greater depth.

Literature Review

Evidence from our district's review of reading programs showed us that teachers were struggling with integrating the arts in meaningful ways into their programs. Our standardized testing data and teacher reports told us that students struggled with some of the language standards such as making connections and point of view. With this information in mind, we decided to focus on these areas. The kindergarten teachers in our group chose to focus on making connections and retelling stories in proper sequence.

From our previous work, we were convinced that Lab Class as a model of teacher inquiry can be a powerful learning model with long-lasting impact on classroom practice and student achievement.

Inquiry positions the teacher as an informed practitioner refining planning, instruction, and assessment approaches in the continual pursuit of greater precision, personalization and innovation. Data generated from student actions and work compels teachers to investigate new, engaging, and relevant questions about how and what their students learn (Ontario Ministry of Education, 2010c).

Our preliminary research review supported the use of drama as a tool for extending students' reading comprehension skills. Research from the Royal Conservatory (n.d.) on their Learning Through The Arts (LTTA) program found that students who participated in learning through the arts were more engaged in their lessons, demonstrated greater recall of both arts and non–arts-related content even years later and were three times more likely to report that they enjoyed going to school.

In December, the entire team met for a full day for our Launch Meeting. Teachers were asked to select five marker students from each class and to track their progress over the course of the project. Teachers meet with same grade colleagues and selected specific curriculum expectations and standards that they wanted to focus on for the inquiry and did some initial planning.

From January to April, teachers met monthly for a half day for classroom observation visits. During each of these sessions, drama in education students from the university provided support with practical classroom strategies related to the mentor texts, to the expectations (making connections, making inferences, and point of view), and to the students' strengths and interests. Some of the drama techniques we explored included corridor of voices, hot seat, role on the wall, clay sculpting, tableau, graffiti, and soundscapes (Booth, 2005; Booth & Lundy, 1985; Rooyackers, 1998; Shreeves, 1990; Swartz, 2002).

Analyses

Student work

When examining the student work, teachers noted a remarkable improvement in the achievement of all students for the selected curriculum expectations and standards, but especially for those marker students who were not usually strong students. The drama activities allowed the students to formulate ideas, develop vocabulary, and gain the confidence to share. Using drama, students seemed more willing to take risks in their learning. The teachers noted that the students demonstrated "huge" improvement in both receptive and expressive language when talking with their peers and were transferring this vocabulary to a range of contexts including science, gym, and math classes. Drama gave the students a context to use the vocabulary and engaged a wide range of learners, including those kinesthetic learners. The visual arts activities allowed the students to work with and physically manipulate the ideas they were learning about, and this deepened their understanding. Teachers were delighted that students were choosing the retell activities during activity time, when normally they would choose blocks or other centers.

Teacher Reflections

Teacher 1: At first the students felt uncomfortable expressing their feelings about a character or situation. Because this was a French Immersion program, students often did not have the vocabulary, structures, and ease to express themselves. Over the past 2 months all students' ease of expression improved and all took risks when presenting and speaking in front of their peers. I was quite impressed with how much growth took place in all the students in my class and their ability to make connections to characters and particular situations, paying close attention to language and illustrations to recognize various emotions. It really touched my heart to see those students who never take risks to come up and get in the hot seat to become a character. Truly this was worth the trip!!!

In January and again in April we had teacher participants complete the Arts and Literacy Lab Class Survey. At the beginning of the inquiry project, 66% of the teachers agreed or strongly agreed that they felt confident in their ability to facilitate drama activities and 77% reported that they felt confident in their ability to facilitate visual arts activities. By the end of the inquiry, both responses were at 90%.

Teachers reported that this inquiry project had a profound effect on their teaching and at the regional sharing session one teacher looked at us and said, "I've always used the arts in teaching but now I do it so much better and I understand why I need to do it. My teaching will never be the same." Another teacher wrote,

> The importance of including the arts into other areas is not only that it benefits the students learning, it motivates them as well. They seem to be very engaged in arts activities, and when it is connected to a literacy activity, there is a higher percentage of comprehension.

Future Directions

Reflective Practice and Collaboration

Being provided with release time allowed teachers to meet monthly throughout the project. Teachers identified that being provided with this release time was very valuable and allowed them to work together effectively. Looking at the assessment data as a team assisted in changing teaching practice; teachers modified their expectations for some students because of data analysis and discussion with colleagues. We also found it very valuable to collaborate with the drama in education students from the university. Their expertise and enthusiasm was invaluable to the success of this inquiry project. In the future, we hope to continue this collaboration.

Cross-Curricular Connections

When the project first began, the teachers were quite excited after our Launch Meeting to see what impact the integration of drama and visual arts would have on students' reading achievement. What we found was that not only does the integration of the arts improve achievement, but one of the ways it does that is by increasing student engagement.

Teachers report that they are more likely to integrate the arts, not only with language, but with other subject areas as well. A teacher wrote,

> One key piece of learning from this inquiry is that I have looked at teaching and learning in a while new way. I feel that the arts are a very valuable part of a student's learning and should be taught more often in cross-curricular ways.

Teacher Support

In our review of both the pre- and post-survey anecdotal comments, the teachers repeatedly stated that they wanted more support on how to integrate the arts into the program and more resources for arts integration. Yet in the data in the survey questions, 90% said they felt confident in their ability to facilitate drama activities and visual arts activities, 70% felt confident in their abilities to facilitate dance activities, and only 50% felt confident in their abilities to facilitate music activities. On one hand teachers are indicating that they feel confident implementing some of the arts, yet they are still at a point in the development of their skills where scaffolds and support are desired.

In the post-inquiry survey, teachers said:

- I would be motivated to use the arts more often if I had more resources in my classroom.
- Developing these integrated lessons is where I need the support and help to generate those ideas to then deliver them to my students.
- I would be motivated to use the arts more often if someone showed me (visually) and went over step-by-step how to deliver new lessons and techniques.

As educational leaders, we must consider how to provide more effective support to teachers and students. Some strategies may include providing more resources in schools, scheduling after school workshops with practical strategies for classroom implementation, and purchasing professional resources for schools, as well as hands-on materials for drama and visual arts. We are also looking at continuing this focus on the arts and literacy in next year's Lab Class project, and perhaps expanding to additional schools, depending on funding.

Continuing our partnership with the university drama in education program is another way we can provide practical strategies and step-by-step mentoring for teachers.

Teachers in our immersion schools also found it difficult to find mentor texts that were rich enough to spark interesting drama experiences for the students and yet had a vocabulary that was not too challenging for the students. Working together with the Teacher Consultant responsible for our French programs, as well as the instructional coach, we plan to purchase additional mentor texts as funds become available.

Survey

Question 1: I consider myself a creative person.

PRETEST N=9 POSTTEST N=10	STRONGLY AGREE	AGREE	DISAGREE	STRONGLY DISAGREE
Response % Response Count	22.2 2	55.6 5	11.1 1	11.1 1
Response % Response Count	10.0 1	40.0 4	40.0 4	10.0 1

Question 2: I feel confident in my ability to facilitate drama activities.

PRETEST N=9 POSTTEST N=10	STRONGLY AGREE	AGREE	DISAGREE	STRONGLY DISAGREE
Response % Response Count	11.1 1	55.6 5	22.2 2	11.1 1
Response % Response Count	0.0 0	90.0 9	10.0 1	0.0 0

Question 3: I feel confident in my ability to facilitate dance activities.

PRETEST N=9 POSTTEST N=10	STRONGLY AGREE	AGREE	DISAGREE	STRONGLY DISAGREE
Response % Response Count	11.1 1	66.7 6	11.1 1	11.1 1
Response % Response Count	10.0 1	60.0 6	30.0 3	0.0 0

Question 4: I feel confident in my ability to facilitate music activities.

PRETEST N=9 POSTTEST N=10	STRONGLY AGREE	AGREE	DISAGREE	STRONGLY DISAGREE
Response % Response Count	11.1 1	44.4 4	22.2 2	22.2 2
Response % Response Count	10.0 1	40.0 4	40.0 4	10.0 1

Question 5: I feel confident in my ability to facilitate visual arts activities.

PRETEST N=9 POSTTEST N=10	STRONGLY AGREE	AGREE	DISAGREE	STRONGLY DISAGREE
Response % Response Count	11.1 1	66.7 6	11.1 1	11.1 1
Response % Response Count	40.0 4	50.0 5	10.0 1	0.0 0

Question 6: I feel that I don't have enough time to teach the arts along with the rest of the curriculum.

PRETEST N=9 POSTTEST N=10	STRONGLY AGREE	AGREE	DISAGREE	STRONGLY DISAGREE
Response % Response Count	22.2 2	22.2 2	44.4 4	11.1 1
Response % Response Count	0.0 0	50.0 5	50.0 5	0.0 0

Question 7: My students have trouble concentrating on other work after an arts activity.

PRETEST N=9 POSTTEST N=10	STRONGLY AGREE	AGREE	DISAGREE	STRONGLY DISAGREE
Response % Response Count	0.0 0	22.2 2	77.8 7	0.0 0
Response % Response Count	0.0	30.0 3	70.0 7	0.0

Question 8: I feel that I have enough resources to incorporate the arts into my classroom.

PRETEST N=9 POSTTEST N=10	STRONGLY AGREE	AGREE	DISAGREE	STRONGLY DISAGREE
Response % Response Count	11.1 1	33.3 3	44.4 4	11.1 1
Response % Response Count	10.0 1	40.0 4	50.0 5	0.0

Question 9: I feel that many students in my class would benefit from more arts activities in the curriculum.

PRETEST N=9 POSTTEST N=10	STRONGLY AGREE	AGREE	DISAGREE	STRONGLY DISAGREE
Response % Response Count	33.3 3	66.7 6	0.0 0	0.0 0
Response % Response Count	40.0 4	60.0 6	0.0	0.0 0

Question 10: Please share your ideas around the following statements: My current motivation for using the arts in my teaching is . . . I would be motivated to use the arts more often if . . .

Pretest comments (6 answered the question; 3 skipped the question)

1. I would be motivated to use the arts more often if I had some practical ideas that I could readily use. It's great to link art activities into favorite picture books.
2. I believe art is an important part of the curriculum.

3. Research indicates that learning curriculum concepts is enhanced if art is included in the learning activities. I would be motivated to use the arts more if I had more resources.
4. I feel the arts are important to a child's social, emotional, and intellectual development.
5. I would be motivated to use the arts more if I had more resources and experts in the field to visit my classroom and help facilitate the program.
6. I used arts in my teaching occasionally. I do not feel I have enough resources or experience to teach this. I would be more motivated if I had prepared lessons that would walk me through step by step.

Posttest comments (9 answered the question, 1 skipped the question)

1. My current motivation for using the arts in my teaching is to capture the interest of more of my students based on their abilities and learning needs. I would be motivated to use the arts more often if I had someone who was qualified to come into my classroom and model for me what to do and how to teach the arts on a regular basis. I am a visual and kinesthetic learner and require that hands on approach. One key piece of learning from this inquiry is that I looked at teaching and learning in a whole new way. I feel that the arts are a valuable part of a students' learning and should be taught more often in a cross-curricular way. Developing those lesson plans is where I need the support and help to generate those ideas to then deliver to my students. I would benefit from having an expert to co-teach with for a few weeks.
2. My current motivation for using the arts in my teaching is that now I actually know about the professional resources available in my building. In addition, I have been given and shown and participated in some practical art and drama activities throughout the course of this inquiry.
3. One key piece of learning is the results we have seen—the students' ability to respond has increased.
4. Arts definitely helps students understand second language and helps students make connections. I would love to have a few more resources for drama. This has definitely improved my students' ability to read French and make connections to the text.
5. To better engage students in all subjects by using the arts.
6. My current motivation for using the arts in my teaching is to improve the oral language of my students. I would be motivated to use the arts more often if I had resources in my classroom and if I had more time to teach it. One key piece of learning for me is to use arts in conjunction with language and more specifically reading to improve student achievement.

7. I learned about how the arts compliment the curriculum. The importance of including the arts into other areas of the curriculum not only benefits the students' learning, but it motivates them as well. They seem to be very engaged in arts activities, and when it is connected to literacy there is a higher percentage of comprehension.
8. One key piece of learning for me is that the arts should be an integral part of the curriculum but as many people do not necessarily feel confident in teaching the arts, experts should be available to facilitate whenever necessary. I for one have many misconceptions about the different areas of the arts and would benefit from time and expertise to develop my program to incorporate the arts so that it is meaningful not only for me but for my students as well.
9. My current motivation for using the arts in my teaching is curriculum-driven. I would be motivated to use the arts more often if someone showed me and went over step-by-step how to deliver new lessons and techniques. One key piece of learning for me was that my students enjoy incorporating the arts into their daily work.

Survey questions adapted from Oreck, (2004).

Lab Class Two: Multiple Teachers/Multiple Schools

Co-investigators and their roles:

NAME OF CO-LEARNERS/ CO-INVESTIGATORS	ROLE	LOCATION
Consultant One	Teacher Consultant	Central Office
Consultant Two	Teacher Consultant	Central Office
Instructional Coach	Coach	Central Office
Teacher One	Kindergarten Teacher	Elm Street PS
Teacher Two	Kindergarten Teacher	Elm Street PS
ECE One	Early Childhood Educator	Elm Street PS
Teacher Three	Grade 1 Teacher	Elm Street PS
Teacher Four	Grades 1 and 2 Teacher	Elm Street PS

NAME OF CO-LEARNERS/ CO-INVESTIGATORS	ROLE	LOCATION
Teacher Five	Grades 2 and 3 Teacher	Elm Street PS
Teacher Six	Special Ed. Teacher Grades 6, 7, and 8	Elm Street PS
Teacher Seven	Primary Teacher	Elm Street PS
Principal One	Principal	Elm Street PS
Teacher Eight	Kindergarten Teacher	Maple Street PS
ECE Two	Early Childhood Educator	Maple Street PS
Teacher Nine	Kindergarten Teacher	Maple Street PS
ECE Three	Early Childhood Educator	Maple Street PS
Teacher 10	Grade 1 Teacher	Maple Street PS
Teacher 11	Grade 2 Teacher	Maple Street PS
Teacher 12	Grade 2 Teacher	Maple Street PS
Principal Two	Principal	Maple Street PS
Teacher 13	Kindergarten Teacher	Oak Street PS
ECE Four	Early Childhood Educator	Oak Street PS
Teacher 14	Grade 1 Teacher	Oak Street PS
Teacher 15	Grade 2 Teacher	Oak Street PS
Teacher 16	Grades 1 and 2 Teacher	Oak Street PS
Teacher 17	Grade 2 Teacher	Oak Street PS
Principal Three	Principal	Oak Street PS
Ministry Staff	Coach	Ministry of Education

Oak Street Public School (PS) is an urban school with an environmental focus. It has a growing population with a current student population of 583 students. It is located in a city with a population of 400,000. The city has a mix of industrial and commercial business, one university and one college, and a large population of recently arrived immigrants.

Elm Street Public School is an urban school with 440 students located in the same city. Elm Street PS is considered a compensatory school with a high number of students from low socioeconomic status (SES) homes, a high English Language Learner population, and a high degree of student transience.

Maple Street Public School is similar to Elm Street PS in that it is also located in the city and is also a compensatory school. The student population is 367 students.

In all three schools the kindergarten teams of teachers and ECEs had been learning more about emergent curriculum and student inquiry through attendance at professional learning sessions at both the district and regional levels, professional reading and dialogue with their colleagues and administrators. They were eager to continue their exploration of student-led inquiry and to share this journey with their colleagues in the primary grades. The administrators at all three schools were also eager to extend inquiry learning beyond the kindergarten classrooms. Additionally, a 3-day summer institute had been offered by the central office consultants, and each of these schools had several teachers from kindergarten and primary who attended and expressed an interest in continuing their learning through Lab Class. This resulted in a final team of five kindergarten teachers, four early childhood educators, four Grade 1 teachers, two Grades 1 and 2 combined teachers, four Grade 2 teachers, one Grades 2 and 3 teacher, one intermediate special education teacher, a coach, and two consultants. In addition, a Ministry of Education coach supported the work of the group by attending sessions when possible and connecting via e-mail and phone.

Inquiry Questions

Oak Street Public School: What is the impact of taking an inquiry stance on students' ability to make and demonstrate meaning?

- If all students know they are valued, then a sense of community will be developed.
- If student voice is considered, then students will take more ownership of their learning.
- If documentation is purposeful, then it will provide assessment for learning to uncover students' strengths, needs, and interests.
- If authentic learning experiences are created then students will engage in a deeper level in their learning.

Elm Street Public School: What is the impact of intentionally creating an inquiry learning environment that provokes student action, dialogue, and reflection on students' expression of their learning?

- If a provocation space or station were made available in the classroom, then students will ask higher order questions.

- If higher order questions are modeled and explicitly taught, then students will ask higher order questions of each other.
- If higher level question stems are generated, practiced, and posted, then students will learn to ask higher level questions.
- If educators collaborate to brainstorm ongoing provocations to expand existing inquiries, then students will produce higher level responses.
- If educators use novel materials, texts, and learning opportunities linked to curriculum to provoke inquiry, then students will demonstrate curricular expectations in expressions of their learning.
- If educators monitor student interest in learning opportunities and aim to maintain this interest, then students will demonstrate increased knowledge in expressions of their learning.

Maple Street Public School: What is the impact of explicitly teaching oral language on students' confidence and ability to express their thoughts, ideas, and questions within an inquiry-based environment?

- If students are explicitly taught to reflect and think critically about their ideas, thoughts, and questions, then they will see the value of their ideas and have the confidence to share their ideas with others.
- If teachers provide students with multiple and varied opportunities to share their reflections and observations of their learning with others, then they will see themselves as effective communicators.
- If teachers provide students with multiple and varied opportunities to share their reflections and observations of their learning with others, then they will engage more effectively as learners.

What Are We Learning From Research?

We used a Lab Class model that focused on observing students, analyzing those observations to look for patterns and supporting conditions, and then focusing our learning on what we had learned from our observation of the students.

From our experience as educators, we knew that when students were truly engaged in learning, their motivation, their persistence, their enthusiasm, and their achievement increased. Research suggests that students are more likely to develop as engaged, self-directed learners in inquiry-based classrooms (Jang, Reeve, & Deci, 2010, in Ontario Ministry of Education, 2011). As we embarked on deepening our understanding of the impact of inquiry on engagement and on the students' ability to communicate their thinking, we considered not only inquiry as a whole but also some of the important conditions necessary for inquiry to occur. Many of the resources we used at the beginning of our work this year were the same as our group last year, because they grappled with some of the same issues and concerns.

The power of an inquiry-based approach to teaching and learning is its potential to increase intellectual engagement and foster deep understanding through the development of a hands-on, minds-on, and "research-based disposition" toward teaching and learning. Inquiry honors the complex, interconnected nature of knowledge construction, striving to provide opportunities for both teachers and students to collaboratively build, test, and reflect on their learning. This view of inquiry learning fit with our view of teaching and learning as multilayered and multifaceted, with connections between content areas as well as between all the learners, adult and children, in the classroom. Through our discussions, experience, and readings we were forced to reconsider the role of the teacher and the role of the student.

> Sometimes discussions about education treat teaching and learning as almost synonymous. In reality, the conditions and goals of the one who teaches are not identical to the conditions and goals of the one who learns. After all we have said about children, we have to discuss more fully the role that children assume in the construction of self and knowledge, and the help they get in these matters from adults. It is obvious that between learning and teaching, we honor the first. It is not that we ostracize teaching, but we tell it, "Stand aside for a while and leave room for learning, observe carefully what children do, and then, if you have understood well, perhaps teaching will be different than before" (Malaguzzi in Edwards, Gandini, & Forman, 2012).

We examined the types of questions that we and our students were asking of themselves and each other about their topics of investigation. Wien (2008) argues that

> thinking of questions as "seeds to thinking" rather than queries requiring answers is a major change in a teacher's teaching practice. If the question is a seed, it is asked for a different purpose than receiving a correct answer; it is asked to stimulate thinking and feeling. To be asked, "What do you think?" is a very different engagement than being asked for an answer. (p. 43)

One of our challenges when beginning the journey with inquiry for educators in the grades beyond kindergarten were the beliefs that teachers held about our standardized curriculum with its lists of both overall and specific expectations. Wien (2004) has documented that this format leads teachers to the unintended interpretation that items must be taught item by item. Time and again, educational leaders and facilitators hear concerns from teachers, parents, and administrators about the need to "cover the curriculum." Wien (2008) states that

> the explicit and direct instruction of a linear, fragmented approach is one way to teach a standardized curriculum. For young children, it is not the

> best approach, for it contravenes the research knowledge bases of child development and neuroscience. Another way to teach standardized curriculum is to embed it in richer, more integrated processes such as emergent curriculum, where its presence can be documented to make it visible, rather than being measured on tests. (p. 158)

As our project progressed, the team members were encouraged and motivated by the students' enthusiasm for learning when engaged in inquiry. Their natural curiosity and inquisitiveness drove them to explore ideas and issues that were meaningful and relevant to them in a real-world context. As teachers nurture this natural inquisitiveness through an inquiry approach, "they are enabling students to address curriculum content in integrated and 'real world' ways and to develop and practice higher order thinking skills and habits of mind that lead to deep learning" (Ontario Ministry of Education, 2011).

The Lab Class model helped participants focus on the students, their learning, their thinking and the conditions present that were supporting the learning. As we progressed we began to more closely examine the purpose and impact of documenting student learning. We explored the stages of documentation, ethical issues around documenting student learning, and varying opinions on this subject. Loris Malaguzzi (1994) believed that "when the child is observed, the child is happy—it's almost an honor that he is observed by an adult." Yet Pat Tarr (2011) cautioned readers that

> what it means for children to give informed consent is shifting as researchers devise ways to make their research objectives, the use of the data collected, the specifics of what is required of the children and their right to withdraw at any time understandable—even to very young children. We might openly discuss and ask for consent from children before we begin to document, and to consider that this is provisional consent that is continually renegotiated. This requires sensitivity because of inherent power relationships in the teacher-student relationships to ensure that children know they have a right to say no at any time. No matter how good our intentions are, I believe that we should be mindful of the question "What is our right to do this?" Should our needs as educators to plan curriculum and assess students for reporting purposes override students' right to have a voice in those things that concern them? (p. 15)

The instructional coach in our group was having some concerns about the impact of documentation on students and was conducting informal interviews with some of the students with whom she worked. While she felt that she was making a concerted effort to include students in the process, many expressed reservations about the project and how their learning was being documented. She began to offer the students choice: Would they like to participate, how would they like their learning to be documented (anecdotal notes, video, photographs, etc.), and with whom would the documentation be shared? This had a major impact on not only her work and her beliefs and attitudes about the Lab Class model, but also student documentation in general. We may believe that we have been considerate of students' thoughts, ideas, and feelings; however, it is imperative that we as teacher-researchers dig deeper to engage our students and uncover their understandings of this ethical dilemma.

As time passed, we also began to reexamine the types of provocations that we were using to engage the students and uncover their prior knowledge and existing understandings. Our provocations became simpler ("what do you know about measurement?") and yet yielded rich data and multifaceted questions that could guide further investigation. This was one area where we found a lack of professional resources and gathered ideas from conversations with other educators in our board and beyond.

> Each one of us needs to be able to play with the things that are coming out of the world of children. Each one of use needs to have curiosity, and we need to be able to try something new based on the ideas that we collect from the children as they go along. Life has to be somewhat agitated and upset, a bit restless, somewhat unknown. As life flows with the thoughts of the children, we need to be open, we need to change our ideas; we need to be comfortable with the restless nature of life. All of this changes the role of the teacher, a role that becomes much more difficult and complex. It also makes the world of the teacher more beautiful, something to become involved in. (Malaguzzi, 1994, p. 2)

Or as one of our administrators more succinctly put it, "We have to get comfortable with being uncomfortable."

What Are We Learning From Educators in the Field?

This year, we wanted to explore Lab Class as a school-based learning model with multiple participants from one school working and learning together. We met four times as a whole group with all three schools; we called these meetings our Networked Learning Sessions. Between each whole group session, we asked the schools to select a half day to engage in an in-school Lab Class model. We wanted to determine if this Lab Class model could be sustained at a school level and would be an option for principals when they are determining how to use their professional learning community time. Each of the three central office staff involved in this project was aligned with one of the participating schools and engaged in the learning at the school level. At one of our schools the administrator decided to "top up" the funding and have a full-day Lab Class for each in-school session; at the other two schools, it remained a half-day release session.

The Lab Class participants used our analysis of what students were saying and doing to determine our next steps for professional learning. The link between the classroom experience and the pedagogy was evident to all participants.

Educator quotes:

- "At our last Lab Class, my class was observed. At the feedback, I was happy to hear that one of my weakest students was completing the activity successfully and reaching higher level thinking. Inquiry has allowed me to see the growth in my students by focusing on their oral contributions."
- Pivotal Moment: "Giving myself permission to let go of components of my Kindergarten Program that weren't academically high yield, but fun, in favor of inquiry-based projects, which both student and teacher get more out of."
- "A moment when I realize I may have shortchanged a child by doubting what they are capable of. My appreciation comes when I can accept my downfall and receive positive support from my partners in education to move forward to *be* better so that I may *do* better."

Kindergarten student quote:

- "You're here with the other teachers? (yes) Excuse me, I need to go share with them."

What Documentation and Evidence Communicates Your Team's Learning to Others?

Oak Street Public School—What Evidence and Why?

Student Learning

We collected a variety of student work products using photographs and compiled it with the connected documentation of what students said and did through our recorded observations and conversations with and of the students. We believe that due to this triangulation of data we have a clearer picture of what students understand and any misconceptions that they may have.

Student learning clusters that emerged:

- Prior knowledge and sharing
- Making connections
- Multiple ways to represent thinking

- Making meaning
- Classroom resources
- Use of technology
- Peer collaboration
- Metacognition
- Self-confidence
- Student interest
- Self-driven learning (motivation)
- Higher level thinking

Student learning comparison:

- Before our students were using prior knowledge to make connections, and now they are sharing their prior knowledge and connections.
- Before our students were engaging in self-talk, and now they are collaborating with each other to share, defend, and challenge ideas.
- Before our students were independently problem solving, and now they are collaborating.
- Before our students were demonstrating self-regulation, and now they are showing their confidence, self-regulation is a given.
- Now metacognition has emerged.
- Now use of technology has emerged.

Comparison of the Benefits of Inquiry:

- Students still are making meaning of their world using multiple strategies.
- At first, they were becoming aware, and now they are aware that they have knowledge worth sharing.
- Reflecting on their thinking orally (at first, they were becoming and now they are metacognitive).
- Engaging in their environment to construct learning.
- At first, we were building a sense of community, and now together we have established a sense of community to support learning through questioning, guiding, reflecting, challenging, and accepting.
- Scaffolding to support learning at zone of proximal development by paying close attention to our learners (posing questions, conversations, observations, products).

    - At first it was more modeled and shared, and now we are moving into independent and paired.
- Now we and the students value talk and collaboration.

What We Have Learned: Students

- Students have developed a sense of community because they are now working more collaboratively and sharing more of their ideas with each other—students feel valued because their interests are considered and their environment reflects their ideas.
- Students are given opportunities to reflect on their learning to bridge the gaps between earlier concepts and new learning (i.e., students learned about tally marks to vote on a book, and in a future activity, they were able to use tally marks to keep track of student points).
- In making our student voice more visible, we have seen our students take a lot of ownership for their learning (i.e., students have created a seed book to document a growing project; student created a book about the Titanic that he then turned into a play, and he is now creating a movie based on his prior knowledge; students engaged in problem solving to create their own structures, using a variety of materials, to demonstrate stability).
- Our students are making many connections to the real world—transferring their knowledge and skills to real-life experiences. In our experience, we are seeing the reciprocal relationship that inquiry is bringing to our children.
- Our purposeful documentation has provided parents with an opportunity for them to make meaning of their children's learning.
- We have clearly seen our students being more engaged in their learning because they are exposed to truly authentic and meaningful experiences; it is not about our agenda, it's about where the students want to take their learning.

Educator Learning

We filtered all the documentation that was taken during Lab Class for observations that were descriptive and that connected to our inquiry question and/or theory of action statements. We then chose a few key learning moments and transcribed these onto Post-It notes. We clustered these student learning moments and labelled the learning that was being uncovered. We then reflected on the benefits of inquiry that supported the student learning. We kept these charts as artifacts of our professional learning and compared them after each subsequent Lab Class.

What We Have Learned: Educators

- Writing out reflections of our students' experiences (documenting) has allowed us to clearly see the next steps in their learning; being able to revisit these written statements allows us to see how far the students have come or revisit areas of learning as necessary.
- The act of documentation helps keep our viewpoint of the child more purposeful and helps keep us accountable to the student and the learning.
- As educators, we need to have a strong grasp of our curriculum to be the link between where the students are taking their learning and what we need to cover in the curriculum.
- We have discovered that the more excited we are about their learning, the more excited they will be; we can model that we don't have all the answers and it is about the process of discovery. It is sometimes uncomfortable to let the control go and be accepting of the fact that we might not always get to the right answer like in a traditional model.
- The inquiry process naturally involves the family as well because the students go home requesting materials or talking about what they are learning and wanting to research more and bringing what they know from home back to their learning at school.
- Parents are sharing that they see that their children are engaged in the learning at home as well.
- We have learned that inquiry doesn't evolve overnight, and we've discovered that our unique personalities and traits can impact how we implement it in the classroom.
- One educator's pivotal moment: "I've taught Gr. 1 for two years and when I thought back to last year I wondered why I didn't see the same level of self-regulation in the students. Both years they were coming from the same great inquiry based Kindergarten program, what was the big difference? Upon reflection, I realized that the difference was me!"

Implications of Our Learning

- From working together, we have learned that we have some common struggles and we are able to learn from each other, so we are more effective having the team element.
- We have discovered that there are some differences in how the inquiry looks in the early years compared to the primary years based on the curriculum.
- The way we use the documentation binders needs to be made more accessible for the students, thereby increasing the ownership even more.

Elm Street Public School—What Evidence and Why?

Student Learning

Student work/artifacts, photos, videos, observational notes of student action, conversation, and product. We collected this evidence because we felt this variety and range of evidence would paint a clear picture of student learning.

These themes came out frequently throughout this study

- Identified stages of inquiry
- Demonstrated perseverance
- Independently referenced cues, tools, and artifacts in the classroom
- Felt free to make choices
- Collaborated with peers
- Researched and extended the inquiry
- Initiated further inquiry
- Engaged in oral communication
    - Reflective of high level thinking
    - To problem solve
    - To reflect on their learning
- Engaged in written communication
    - To ask questions
    - To reflect on their learning
- Made connections to prior learning and personal experiences

Educator Learning

We kept the charts we created to hold the observational notes taken during Lab Class. On these charts, you can see the clusters and themes we determined based on what we noticed in student learning.

We also kept our Conditions Present chart that was created following the analysis and clustering of the Lab Class observations, as follows:

Conditions Present

- Routines clearly established.
- Self-regulation encouraged.

- Student-directed time is embedded in the daily schedule.
- The environment is differentiated.
- Classroom is well-organized, not cluttered, with easy access to materials.
- Stages of inquiry are explicitly taught and visually displayed.
- Opportunities for nonfiction writing are present and varied.
- Frequent and varied opportunities for accountable talk exist.
- Classroom culture allows for risk taking and student ownership of learning.
- Respectful collaboration has been modeled, scaffolded, and encouraged.
- An inquiry stance has been modeled, scaffolded, and encouraged.

Opportunities exist for students to share what they have learned and strategies they have used with peers.

Limitations and Challenges:

- You can't see everyone all the time; some learning may have been missed.
- Sometimes there was uncertainty about whether or not what was collected was adding to the assessment of student learning

What Have We Learned: Pivotal Moments for Students

- The culture exists where students can generate, ask, and investigate their questions at any time—freedom to explore.
- Oral communication improved.
- Intrinsic motivation—were not completing tasks out of compliance, rather very motivated to investigate and research their ideas.

What Have We Learned: Pivotal Moments for Educators

- Deeper understanding of the stages and components of inquiry.
- Despite the discomfort with the unknown and lack of educator control, we feel the students benefit and, as a result, are motivated to continue along this journey.

- The collaboration not only was a support through the discomfort but also provided ideas, new perspectives, and resources.
- The realization that explicit instruction—in large groups, small groups, and/or individually—is relevant, at the educator's discretion, throughout the inquiry process.
- Educator professional judgment is critical in an inquiry learning environment.

Implications of Student Learning on Change in Educator Practice

- Moving toward educator as observer and facilitator as opposed to educator-directed learning engaged and motivated the students to a much higher degree.
- Through following student interest, we found that we were still able to collect relevant assessment data.

As a collaborative team working and learning together we have learned the following:

- It's easier to go on an uncomfortable journey as a team as opposed to on your own.
- Having colleagues into our classrooms in this nonjudgmental way was informative and supportive.
- The trust in the group allowed for greater comfort, risk taking, and a more open dialogue.

Implications for Further Actions or Further Questions

We are considering exploring the following in an inquiry environment:

- Perseverance
- Varying level of structure for different learners
- The possibility of two or more inquiries going on at one time in the classroom
- The relationship between asking higher level questions and learning in inquiry environments

Maple Street Public School—What Evidence and Why?

Student Learning

Student work, photos of student work and student collaboration, Post-It notes with teacher observations of student learning sorted by categories, anecdotal notes, student oral language logs, photos of student work, samples of student talk, and photos of documentation panels. Collecting this evidence helped us focus on the students and their learning, as well as our own professional learning.

- Noticed that some students needed explicit teaching about inquiry.
- From sharing sessions, the educators noticed a change in the questions that students asked.
- Sharing their learning had an interesting impact: Students were motivated to share their knowledge because they knew that they had an attentive audience; students focused on how to organize their work so others could understand; they really understood that speaking, writing, and presenting their ideas was for the purpose to communicate a message.
- We realized that we couldn't assume that students had the vocabulary to express their ideas, and educators used that moment to use prompts and encouragement to help students find their words.

Educator Learning

Post-It notes of teacher observations of student learning sorted by categories, photos of student work, and photos of documentation panels with educator annotation. We also created an Evernote page, which tracked our project chronologically with notes and photos.

- We had to determine what level of scaffolding was necessary for each student to engage in the inquiry process successfully.
- Stages of inquiry needed to be explicitly taught and displayed in the classroom.

Limitations and Challenges:

We found that as time progressed, our sorting of the student observation data changed as our comfort level with inquiry grew and our focus shifted from inquiry to a broader scope.

Some educators wondered what it would look like to have a control group for comparison as part of our inquiry.

What We Have Learned and Pivotal Moments for Students:

- Students have learned that they learn from asking questions and that asking questions helps them with their learning.
- Students see value in their sharing.
- Students seem more willing to share when they feel that someone will be learning from their experience.
- Students are able to listen with a purpose.

What We Have Learned and Pivotal Moments for Educators:

- Aha moments when students notice something and have the ability to describe and explain. Their pride is noticeable as well as their confidence.
- We found that when we helped students think about how they learned best, we could provide tiered instruction with opportunities for independent research, "sit and get," and reading books,
- Students needed support to ask questions and take responsibility or ownership of the learning.
- Students needed explicit teaching of the inquiry process. We engaged in the four steps of inquiry, and students learned their ideas could be explored and further questioned.
- Educator quote: In the classroom I usually run manically from one child to another to photograph a document. Valentine's Day I decided to stay next to one child for a very long time. Really converse, really listen, and take many pics of one child working very hard and documenting his thinking. Not only did I get a great learning story but I also learned details that I never would have from this little guy had I moved one child to another.

What's Next?

During the regional meeting in May with teams from 15 other school districts, the participants spoke about the importance of a supportive environment and trusting relationship with colleagues and administrators to move forward with their work with student inquiry. At the beginning, some participants felt uncomfortable with this approach to instruction and needed the support and encouragement to keep going. Had they not had that support, many felt they might have given up. We are looking at ways to continue to support an inquiry stance for all teachers from kindergarten to Grade 8 and beyond in all schools. They also discussed the importance of feeling that they had "permission" to SLOW DOWN so that they could listen to the students and let the inquiry unfold.

Our plans moving forward include:

Supporting the Lab Class model: We are currently supporting a variety of schools to uncover more about their students' strengths and areas for growth and the connected professional learning opportunities using Lab Class. Schools are exploring the structure of lab class with divisional and cross divisional teams along with cross panel opportunities. For example, at one school a team of educators visits one host classroom over several weeks, collecting observation data on three or four marker students. They then sort the observations, using a different color of sticky note for each marker student, to look for commonalities and determine next steps. In our work with schools, we intend to continue to support administrators and educators in exploring this professional learning model.

Summer Institute: We are offering a summer institute called Real Classrooms! Real Inquiry! Several of the teams from Lab Class as well as from other schools will be sharing their inquiry journeys with their elementary colleagues. The descriptor reads:

> Research suggests that students are more likely to develop as engaged, self-directed learners in inquiry-based classrooms. In this full-day workshop participants will learn what it means to adopt an inquiry stance across the curriculum. Participants will have the opportunity to select from a variety of educator-led stations representing real classroom inquiries from across our system. Examples from kindergarten to Grade 8, including Special Education Resource Room, will be shared. Time will be provided for participants to explore lingering questions and consider how to move forward with inquiry in their classrooms.

After-School Sessions: We offered monthly after-school sessions called Early Primary Networked Learning Community meetings. Each meeting was held at a school, and we began by having the educators share their learning journey with their students. Often it was the kindergarten team, but we invited other primary teachers to share as well. These meetings were received with great enthusiasm, and attendance averaged 50 to 60 participants each month including representatives from our school-based child care providers. Average attendance at after-school workshops is usually 8 to 20 educators, so these attendance levels were exciting.

Lab Class Three: Multiple Schools/One Teacher

Participants:

- Program Consultant
- Coach

- K–1 Teacher 1, School A
- K–1 Teacher 2, School B
- K–1 Teacher 3, School C

This team was formed the second year that our school district had combined kindergarten and Grade 1 classrooms. Teacher 1 had taught K–1 the previous year; Teacher 2 and Teacher 3 were both new to this assignment.

Inquiry Question

What are the instructional strategies that support students in thinking about numbers and expressing their own mathematical thoughts?

Theory of Action

If we use instructional strategies (such as Number Talks, technology, effective questioning and small group instruction) then students will improve in their ability to communicate their mathematical thinking.

Literature Review

We began our inquiry with the belief that our students were capable of deep mathematical thinking but were not able to communicate the range and depth of their thinking to peers, parents, or educators. Several studies reveal that children bring more mathematical knowledge and experience to school than previously believed. In one study, preschool children were observed frequently engaging in a range of mathematics, including pattern and shape, magnitude, enumeration, spatial relations, classification, and dynamic change. Researchers note that children's thinking "is not limited to the concrete and mechanical; it is often complex and abstract" (Ginsburg et al., 2003, p. 236, cited in Ontario Ministry of Education, 2010a).

In the Full-Day Early Learning Kindergarten document, educators are reminded that

> young children come to school already knowing a great deal about mathematics. Children bring with them an intuitive knowledge of mathematics, which they have developed through curiosity about their physical world and through real-life experiences. For example, they bring conceptual understanding from their daily experiences with manipulating objects (e.g., fitting different sizes and shapes of a construction toy together), making comparisons (e.g., "I'm taller than you"), making observations (e.g., "This bag is really heavy"), and asking questions (e.g., "Who is taller?" "Who has more cookies?" "How big is it?"). (Ontario Ministry of Education, 2010b, p. 20)

Ginsberg (1999, cited in Heng & Sudarshan, 2013) notes that children possess basic mathematics concepts and skills and engage readily in mathematics through play and informal learning opportunities. Moreover, young children are capable of dealing with a comprehensive and challenging mathematics curriculum and with genuinely interesting mathematics ideas. We wondered how we as educators could support students in being able to communicate their mathematical thinking. Although we began by considering how to structure a supportive environment, as we talked through our wonderings and things we noticed, we decided to focus on instructional strategies that would support student communication. We had to consider "What is communication? How do students communicate?"

Mathematical communication is an essential process for learning mathematics because through communication, students reflect on, clarify, and expand their ideas and understanding of the mathematical relationships and mathematical arguments (Ontario Ministry of Education, 2005). Students may use a range of strategies to share their mathematical thinking including oral communication, written communication, and physical communication through the use of math manipulatives. By sharing their ideas, students can reflect on, clarify, and extend their understanding of different mathematical concepts and relationships. Communicating their mathematical thinking also allows students to consolidate their own understanding as well as analyze and build on the mathematical thinking and strategies of others.

We wanted to explore instructional strategies that would support students in developing these important communication skills and focused on small group instruction, use of technology, use of teachers' prompts and questions, Number Talks, and using manipulatives. Research indicates that these are all powerful strategies for supporting development of student communication.

Small Group Instruction

Small group instruction is a strategy that teachers are comfortable with using for guided reading, and Marilyn Burns (2005) suggests it is also appropriate for mathematics instruction:

> In order to assess children's understanding of mathematical concepts, educators need to ask open-ended questions and engage in sustained conversations that provide opportunities for students to take the lead. Interactions of this nature are **best suited to small-group activities.** . . . it becomes possible for educators to identify the mathematical concepts and strategies that children use for their mathematical reasoning. Collaborating with children during mathematical assessment helps inform intentional teaching strategies and supports ideas for planning effective learning experiences.

Use of Technology

Although our students were adept at using iPads, we wanted to think about how we could use them to increase students' communication about their mathematical thinking. Applications (apps) that are specifically designed for mathematics often focus on a drill and practice approach that simply replaces a worksheet with a worksheet with animation and/or color. Some math apps are games with little opportunity for students to develop problem-solving skills or reflect on their learning (Attard, 2013). Instead we chose to focus on apps that students could use to communicate their thinking, so these may or may not be mathematics apps. Using Chatterbox, students could take photos of the manipulatives that they had used, give the manipulatives a digital mouth, and then record themselves explaining how they used the manipulative to solve the problem. The app would then show the manipulative "speaking" and explaining the math. Use of apps like Explain Everything, Show and Tell, Book Creator, and PicCollage were used to record student thinking, and then share with others both in the school and at home.

Effective Teacher Prompts and Questioning

Klibanoff and colleagues (cited in Ontario Ministry of Education, 2011) found that teacher-facilitated "math talk" in the early years significantly increased children's growth in understanding of mathematical concepts. They noted that young children may have a beginning understanding of mathematical concepts, yet they often lack the language to communicate their ideas. By modeling and fostering math talk throughout the day and across subject areas, educators can provide the math language that allows students to articulate their ideas. To facilitate mathematical thinking rather than direct it, teachers must recognize when student thinking is developing or stalled. If it is developing, the educator observes but leaves the students to work through their thinking (Sarama & Clements, 2009, p. 325, cited in Ontario Ministry of Education, 2011). If it is stalled, probing questions can be asked that provoke thinking about alternate ways to perceive the problem.

Some strategies teachers may employ to provoke thinking include coaching students on how to participate in mathematical discussions (e.g., questioning, explaining, probing one another's mathematical reasoning), developing from and expanding on students' mathematical solutions to make explicit mathematical concepts and strategies related to the lesson's goal, creating mathematical visual records of the class discussion for all students to see, and using mathematical notation to record students' mathematical thinking—a way for primary students to learn that "writing is thinking, written down" (Ontario Ministry of Education, 2010a).

Number Talks

Number Talks (Parrish, 2010) is a resource for teachers from kindergarten to Grade 5 that supports teachers in engaging students in classroom conversations around purposefully crafted computation problems that children solve using mental math. The problems are designed to elicit specific strategies that focus on number relationships and number theory. Number Talks can be done in small group or large group settings. Students solve the problems on their own and then are expected to share and defend their strategies and solutions. This allows students to collaboratively build understanding of mathematics while building connections to key concepts. Number Talks are brief and can usually be conducted in 5 to 15 minutes. The teacher notes clearly explain the strategy that is expected to emerge as well as other, less efficient, strategies that students may use. Teachers are instructed to honor these less efficient strategies while noting connections between their thinking and more efficient strategies.

Manipulatives

Students need the opportunity to learn by doing, talking, and reflecting on their actions through the use of manipulatives in mathematics. Concrete manipulatives provide students with tactile experiences to help them model, describe, and explore mathematics. The Report of the Expert Panel on Early Math in Ontario (Ontario Ministry of Education, 2003) stresses the need for teachers to provide support for their students through the use of manipulatives. When planning activities with manipulatives, the authors of the report advise that teachers should:

- use a manipulative in such a way that students use it as a "thinking tool" enabling them to think about and reflect on new ideas;
- recognize that individual students may use the manipulative in different ways . . . ;
- avoid activities that simply ask children to copy the actions of the teacher;
- allow students to use manipulatives to justify their solution as well as solve the problem; . . . [and]
- provide opportunities for students to explore the same concept with a variety of manipulatives. (p. 20)

Other research that informed our practice was around effective professional learning communities. Katz (2008) reminds us that, to be effective, learning communities must move beyond "story sharing" and into the area of cognitive dissonance and discomfort. While it was important for us to have time to share strategies, we knew we had to move deeper and examine student work to maximize the learning for teachers and students. Lucy West (2012) encourages teachers to take a learning stance and deprivatize our practice. This deprivitization of teacher practice can lead teachers to building new knowledge and problem solving together.

Methodology

To triangulate data, we collected information through observation, conversations, and student work samples from four marker students in each of the three classes. Teachers interviewed the marker students pre- and post-collaborative inquiry on their beliefs and attitudes about mathematics using an interview form that we developed as a group (see Template A). The survey included open response and Likert scale questions.

In their classroom, each teacher recorded their observations in the manner that they preferred including anecdotal notes, photographs, and digital recording using the iPad. These observations were shared in our meetings and online using OneNote. OneNote was also used to share personal reflections on the inquiry journey and student learning and to share the minutes from our meetings.

During our meetings, each teacher shared strategies that they were using to assist students in communicating about mathematics and each teacher chose which strategies they wanted to investigate. We shared samples of student work, observations of our students, responses and questions from parents, and our own reflections on student learning. We also read and discussed professional literature that supported us and sometimes challenged us in our thinking about students and their ability to communicate their mathematical thinking. The conversations during these meetings were rich and engaging and were documented in the minutes for later reflection. Our meetings were held at the schools so we could observe the host's class each meeting. The other two teachers brought videos of their marker students to use for analysis.

Results

Student Learning

From our observations, conversations, and student work we noted an improvement in students' ability and confidence in communicating their mathematical thinking. During the post-collaborative inquiry interviews, marker students seemed more confident when speaking with the teachers, their answers were more detailed, and they had much more to say than in the earlier interview. We also noted during the post-interview that students named specific strategies and specific manipulatives that they were using in their work.

Teachers observed that marker students used math vocabulary when speaking and their number sense vocabulary transferred to other areas of math (e.g., Number Talks strategies were used by the students when communicating and thinking in other areas of math, like patterning). Earlier in the year the students often answered "I don't know" when asked to explain their thinking or actions in math. As our work progressed, teachers noted that students could notice and explain what they were doing, they could identify strategies and the kinds of math they were engaged in, and the use of "I don't know" decreased significantly.

Teacher Learning:
What Did We Learn? What Changed in Our Practice?

As a result of participating in Lab Class, teachers reported that they slowed down and spent more time getting to know and understand the mathematics curriculum. They noticed that they were sometimes teaching "beyond" the curriculum, covering concepts that were beyond the K–1 curriculum expectations. Once they noticed this, they become more thoughtful about what they were teaching and spent more time focusing on key K–1 concepts such as ensuring the students had a solid understanding of 10 by using 10 frames, counting games, Number Talks, subitizing activities, and so on.

Teachers noted that Number Talks (Parrish, 2010) had an immediate impact on their students' confidence in math. Number Talks helped the teachers build community as the students guided each other, the students collaborated, they talked about math strategies, and they developed the mathematical vocabulary to describe what they were doing. Teachers felt that the development of mental math strategies was important in building student confidence in communicating their mathematical thinking.

In our early surveys, students reported that they seldom talked about math at home or at school with their friends. Their answers to the interview questions indicated that they thought of numbers and operations when they thought of math, and we wondered if their parents had the same narrow definition of "What is math?" We realized we needed to be explicit with parents and students about the wide range of math—geometry, patterning, spatial reasoning, measurement, and so on. Teachers were very purposeful in being inclusive of all types of math when communicating with parents and students about mathematics as the inquiry progressed and made an effort to include a wider range of math activities to send home for interested families.

Additionally, because of participation in this inquiry teachers reported that they were spending more time on small group instruction in mathematics, providing more scaffolding for students instead of moving from large group teacher modeling directly to partner work or independent work. They also found that math was more fun—for them and for the students—as they included hands-on learning and child-directed, play-based learning. Being K–1 classrooms, the teachers felt they had more leeway to use play-based learning. If they had a straight Grade 1 class, they reported that there was more pressure from parents to focus on "academics" and less support for play-based learning. However, after this experience, all three teachers indicated that if they were to return to a Grade 1 teaching assignment they would incorporate more child-directed play-based learning in their program after seeing the positive impact it had on their marker students this year.

Conclusion and Discussion

Our theory of action was if we use instructional strategies (such as Number Talks, technology, effective questioning, and small group instruction) then students will improve in their ability to communicate their mathematical thinking, and indeed we found that a range of instructional strategies were found to have a positive impact on the ability for students to communicate thinking. Number Talks (Parrish, 2010) had a profound impact on students' confidence and ability to explain their thinking about numbers. Number Talks also supported teachers in naming the math strategies for students and parents and developing a common understanding and common math vocabulary for communicating our thinking. Number Talks also helped teachers build a community where students and teachers felt safe to share their thinking about math and where it was okay to be wrong.

Using technology was an effective tool for supporting students in communicating their thinking about numbers as we used the technology to help make the mathematics visible and to make their thinking visible. It was easier for some students to communicate their ideas using apps like Show and Tell, Pic Collage, and Chatter Pix because they had a concrete representation of their thinking and/or their work to refer to when they were talking. We also used the SmartBoard to make math visual and support students in communicating their math thinking.

We found that small group instruction was helpful for supporting students in communicating their thinking about number. In the small group setting, students felt safe sharing their thinking, it was easier to ensure all voices were heard, and teachers were able to support and scaffold student learning and understanding. Small group instruction also allowed teachers to more accurately assess student understanding and communication and as a result, give more precise and personalized feedback and plan effective next steps for each student.

Effective questioning was embedded in all that we were doing—Number Talks, using technology, and small group instruction. By focusing on their questioning, teachers could support students in communicating their thinking, uncover students' understanding and misconceptions, and expand on students' mathematical solutions and make connections to specific mathematical concepts and strategies.

All the teacher participants expressed how helpful it was to be part of this inquiry project, because we became a supportive group with whom they could share their observations, their wonderings, and even their frustrations and misgivings. Our theory of action was open-ended enough that each of them felt they could approach it in a way that met their professional learning needs and the needs and strengths of their students.

Baseline Questions for Marker Students

Student: ______________________ Date: ______________________

1. How do mathematicians show their thinking?	
2. Tell me about you and math.	
3. What is math?	
4. Do you like to share about math in big groups?	☹ 😐 ☺
5. Do you like to share about math in small groups?	☹ 😐 ☺
6. Do you like using technology to share your ideas in math?	☹ 😐 ☺
7. Do you like to share your ideas using paper and pencil?	☹ 😐 ☺
8. Do you like to use manipulatives to share your math ideas?	☹ 😐 ☺
9. Do you talk about math at home?	☹ 😐 ☺
10. Do you talk about math with your friends?	☹ 😐 ☺

Final Thoughts

The purpose of this book is to provide readers with an explicit, scaffolded approach for engaging in professional learning through Lab Class. The examples provided throughout the book are intended to act as a model for implementation. The following elements will support those educators engaged in learning collaboratively using the Lab Class model:

- Dedicated time to engage in Lab Class
- Support from school administration and central office staff
- Facilitation by school coaches, consultants, or other teacher leaders
- Access to professional learning resources
- Opportunities for participants to reflect on their learning and share with interested stakeholders including teachers, students, parents, trustees, and others.

Following the steps in this book and creating the conditions described above will not guarantee that Lab Class participants will be successful. Teachers are the heart of Lab Class. They help ensure success through their active engagement in the process: observing their students, questioning their own practice, reading professional literature and resources, sharing their challenges, and reflecting on their learning as well as that of their students.

To the natural born teacher learning is incomplete unless it is shared (Dewey, 2010, p. 35).

Template A

Determine a Focus

STUDENT CAPABILITIES:	STUDENT AREAS FOR GROWTH:

PROFESSIONAL CURIOSITIES:

online resources

Available for download at **resources.corwin.com/LabClass**

Template B

Develop Your Team's Inquiry Question

GOOD INQUIRY QUESTIONS:
• Have deep impact on student learning and educator practice • Generate deep thinking and value multiple perspectives • Provoke action, dialogue, and reflection • Are feasible regarding time, effort, and resources • Are open-ended with many possible answers • Are not based on a commercial resource • Are inclusive of all educators involved • Are something you are GENUINELY curious and passionate about • Are worthy and rich enough to study and research • Require the gathering and analysis of a variety of data over time
WHAT IS THE IMPACT OF (INSTRUCTIONAL PRACTICE RELATED TO INQUIRY) ON (THE IDENTIFIED STUDENT LEARNING NEED)?
Use the space below to begin developing your team's collaborative inquiry question.

Adapted from Ontario Ministry of Education, 2009 [Handout].

Available for download at **resources.corwin.com/LabClass**

Template C

Data Collection for Student Learning

INQUIRY QUESTION:

WHAT EVIDENCE WILL BE COLLECTED?	HOW?	WHEN? BY WHOM?

Adapted from Donohoo for Learning Forward Ontario, (2011).

Available for download at **resources.corwin.com/LabClass**

Template D

Data Collection for Teacher Reflection and Professional Learning

INQUIRY QUESTION:

WHAT EVIDENCE WILL BE COLLECTED?	HOW?	WHEN? BY WHOM?

Adapted from Donohoo for Learning Forward Ontario, (2011).

Available for download at **resources.corwin.com/LabClass**

Template E

Teacher Reflection—Sample One

INQUIRY QUESTION:
PROFESSIONAL CURIOSITIES:
PROFESSIONAL LEARNING:
RESOURCES:
PIVOTAL MOMENTS:
EVIDENCE OF PROFESSIONAL LEARNING:
REFLECTIONS:

online resources Available for download at **resources.corwin.com/LabClass**

Template F

Teacher Reflection—Sample Two

INQUIRY QUESTION:

CURRICULUM EXPECTATIONS AND/OR STANDARDS:

EDUCATOR ACTION	STUDENT LEARNING	DOCUMENTATION

Available for download at **resources.corwin.com/LabClass**

Template G

Teacher Reflection—Sample Three

SCHOOL:		
INQUIRY QUESTION:		
THEORIES OF ACTION:		
INCLUDE EVIDENCE RELATED TO THE GUIDING QUESTIONS	**STUDENT LEARNING**	**EDUCATOR LEARNING**
(Include artifacts and student and educator quotes) • What have you learned? • What were pivotal moments for teachers and students? • What evidence did you collect to address your inquiry question and theory of action statements? • Why that evidence? • What patterns or items of interest did you notice? • Limitations or challenges		
• What are the implications of student learning on change in teacher practice? • What have you learned as a collaborative team about working and learning together? • What are the implications for further actions or further questions?		

Adapted from Ontario Ministry of Education, 2009 [Handout].

Available for download at **resources.corwin.com/LabClass**

Template H

Supports Needed and Next Steps

WHICH IF-THEN STATEMENTS DO YOU WISH TO ENACT?	
WHAT SUPPORT AND/OR RESOURCES MIGHT YOU NEED?	**WITH WHOM MIGHT YOU COLLABORATE?**
CREATE A PLAN FOR THIS WORK:	

online resources Available for download at **resources.corwin.com/LabClass**

Template I

Final Report Template—Sample One

District:

Co-investigators:

Inquiry Question:

INTRODUCTION

Who are you? What are you studying?

In a paragraph or two describe:

- Where the inquiry was conducted
- Your demographic data including any pertinent characteristics of the staff and students
- Your inquiry question, focus of the inquiry, and why it matters to you

LOOKING AT THE RESEARCH (LITERATURE REVIEW)

What does the current policy and research say about your issue or concern?

- What the current policy and research says about your issue
- How the policy and research impacts your inquiry work

DESCRIPTION OF THE INQUIRY PROCESS (METHODOLOGY)

- What did you do?
- Clearly and concisely explain in a paragraph what you did

ANALYSES

What did you find out?

Describe in a few paragraphs what you found out about your inquiry question. You can include:

- Examples of student work
- Reflections on how your practice has changed because of the inquiry
- Statistics, charts, and graphs

FUTURE DIRECTIONS

Describe the implications of your inquiry on your work as educators. How has this impacted your practice? Your beliefs? What do you plan to do next as a part of your teaching practice?

ARTIFACTS

- Quotes from students and/or colleagues (ensure you have written permission from parents and/or colleagues)
- Quotes from a reflective journal
- Quotes from articles, resources
- An excerpt from a learning and/or assessment encounter
- Photographs (ensure you have written permission from parents and/or colleagues)

Adapted from the Ontario Ministry of Education, (2009).

Available for download at **resources.corwin.com/LabClass**

Template J

Final Report Template—Sample Two

School Name:

Participants:

Introduction: Highlight the significance of the problem your group addressed. How did the idea originate? Why was it important to your team? What was the purpose of your inquiry?

Context: Describe the setting. How have you previously tried to address this problem? What are your theories of action?

Method: Elaborate on your theory of action by describing what you did and why. What was the inquiry question? What did the team attempt to accomplish? What were the goals? How did they do it? What evidence did they collect? What successes and challenges did they face?

Findings and Implications: What did your team learn from the investigation? What evidence supports this learning? What, if any, elements of the theory of action were changed? What actions were taken that were not part of the original theory of action?

- What are the implications for student learning?
- What are the implications for teacher learning?

Next Steps and Recommendations: How can you apply what you have learned to further actions? What do you still need to learn about? What is the next step? How will you collect data on the next set of actions?

Adapted from Donohoo for Learning Forward Ontario, (2011).

online resources Available for download at **resources.corwin.com/LabClass**

Template K

Lab Class Feedback—Exit Ticket

Date:

WHAT I CAME EXPECTING . . .	WHAT I GOT . . .
I APPRECIATED . . .	**WHAT I STILL NEED . . .**

online resources Available for download at **resources.corwin.com/LabClass**

Template L

Lab Class Feedback—Survey

Please consider the impact that each of the Lab Class components has had on your professional learning

1—no impact

2—little impact

3—moderate impact

4—strong impact

Developing (and revising) an Inquiry Question:	1 2 3 4
Developing (and revising) Theories of Action:	1 2 3 4
Collecting Evidence of Learning with Marker Students:	1 2 3 4
Observing Students in Other Classes:	1 2 3 4
Teachers Observing My Students:	1 2 3 4
Collaboratively Sorting Lab Class Observations and Identifying Conditions:	1 2 3 4
Professional Reading and Exploring Research:	1 2 3 4
Reflecting and Documenting My Professional Learning:	1 2 3 4

Comments:

Available for download at **resources.corwin.com/LabClass**

References

Adams, L. (n.d.). Learning a new skill is easier said than done. Solana Beach, CA: Gordon Training International. Retrieved from http://www.gordontraining.com/free-workplace-articles/learning-a-new-skill-is-easier-said-than-done/

Argyris, C. (1995). Action science and organizational learning. *Journal of Managerial Psychology, 10*(6), 20–26.

Attard, C. (2013). Teaching with technology—iPads and primary mathematics. *Australian Primary Mathematics Classroom, 18*(4), 38–40.

Bandura, A. (1994). Self-efficacy. In V. S. Ramachaudran (Ed.), *Encyclopedia of human behaviour, 4*, 71–81. New York, NY: Academic Press. Retrieved from https://www.uky.edu/~eushe2/Bandura/BanEncy.html

Bandura, A. (1993). Perceived self-efficacy in cognitive development and functioning. *Educational Psychologist, 28*(2), 117–148.

Blumenfeld, P. C., Marx, R. W., Soloway, E., & Krajcik, J. (1996). Learning with peers: From small group cooperation to collaborative communities. *Educational Researcher, 25*(8), 37–39.

Booth, D. (2005). *Story drama* (2nd ed.). Markham, ON: Pembroke.

Booth, D., & Lundy, C. J. (1985). *Improvisation: Learning through drama.* Toronto, ON: Harcourt Brace Canada.

Burney, D. (2004). Craft knowledge: The road to transforming schools. *Phi Delta Kappan, 85*(7), 526–532.

Burns, (2005). Building a teaching bridge from reading to math. *Leadership Compass, 3*(2), 1–3. Retrieved from https://www.naesp.org/sites/default/files/resources/2/Leadership_Compass/2005/LC2005-06v3n2a1.pdf

Butler, D. L., & Schnellert, L. (2012). Collaborative inquiry in teacher professional development. *Teaching and Teacher Education, 28*, 1206–1220.

Cawsey, T. F., Deszca, G., & Ingols, C. (2016). *Organizational change: An action-oriented toolkit.* Thousand Oaks, CA: Sage.

City, E. A., Elmore, R. F., Fiarman, S. E., & Teitel, L. (2011). *Instructional rounds in education: A network approach to improving teaching and learning.* Cambridge, MA: Harvard Education Press.

Clay, M. M. (2014). *An observation survey of early literacy achievement.* New Zealand: The Marie Clay Literacy Trust.

Datnow, A. (2011). Collaboration and contrived collegiality: Revisiting Hargreaves in the age of accountability. *Journal of Educational Change, 12*(2), 147–158.

Dewey, J. (2010). To those who aspire to the profession of teaching. In D. J. Simpson & S. F. Stack (Eds.), *Teachers, leaders, and schools: Essays by John Dewey.* Carbondale, IL: Southern Illinois University Press.

Donohoo, J. (2013). *Collaborative inquiry for educators: A facilitator's guide to school improvement.* Thousand Oaks, CA: Corwin.

Donohoo, J. (n.d.). *Collaborative Inquiry: A Facilitator's Guide.* Windsor, ON: Learning Forward Ontario.

Edwards, C., Gandini, L., & Forman, G. (2012). *The hundred languages of children: The Reggio Emilia experience in transformation* (3rd ed.). Denver, CO: Praeger.

Fullan, M. (2007). Change the terms for teacher learning. *Journal of Staff Development, 28*(3), 35–36.

Fullan, M. (2001). *Leading in a culture of change*. San Francisco, CA: Jossey-Bass.

Fullan, M., & Hargreaves, A. (2016). *Bringing the profession back in: Call to action*. Oxford, OH: Learning Forward.

Fullan, M., Hill, P., & Crévola, C. (2006). *Breakthrough*. Thousand Oaks, CA: Corwin.

Gadanidis, G., & Hughes, J. M. (2011). Performing big math ideas across the grades. *Teaching Children Mathematics, 17*(8), 486–496.

Groundwater-Smith, S., & Mockler, N. (2009). Inquiry as a framework for professional learning: Interrupting the dominant discourse. *Teacher Professional Learning in an Age of Compliance, 2*, 55–65. Retrieved from http://link.springer.com.proxy1.lib.uwo.ca/book/10.1007%2F978-1-4020-9417-0

Hart, A. W. (1994). Creating teacher leadership roles. *Educational Administration Quarterly*, 30, 472–497.

Heng, M. A., & Sudarshan, A. (2013). "Bigger number means you plus!"—Teachers learning to use clinical interviews to understand students' mathematical thinking. *Educational Studies in Mathematics, 83*(3), 471–485.

Hord, S. M., & Hall, G. E. (2006). *Implementing change: Patterns, principles, and potholes*. New York, NY: Pearson.

Katz, S. (2010). Together is better . . . sometimes: Building and sustaining impactful learning communities within and across schools. *SDCO Connection, 1*(3), 12–13.

Katz, S. (2008). Leaders in educational thought: Special edition on mathematics. Retrieved from https://thelearningexchange.ca/projects/leaders-in-educational-thought-steven-katz-carmel-crevola-anthony-muhammad/?pcat=999&sess=1

Katz, S., & Dack, L. A. (2012). *Intentional interruption: Breaking down learning barriers to transform professional practice*. Thousand Oaks, CA: Corwin.

Katz, S., Dack, L. A., & Earl, L. (2009). Networked learning communities: Fostering learning for teachers and the students. *Principal Connections, 12*(3), 36–38.

Kemmis, S. (1985). Action research and the politics of reflection. In D. Boud, R. Keogh, & D. Walker (Eds.), *Reflection: Turning experience into learning* (pp. 139–141). New York, NY: Kogan Page.

Killion, J. S. (2008). *Assessing impact: Evaluating staff development* (2nd ed.). Thousand Oaks, CA: Corwin.

Leithwood, K., Mascall, B., & Jantzi, D. (2012). Confidence for school improvement: A priority for principals. In K. Leithwood & K. S. Louis (Eds.), *Linking leadership to student learning* (pp. 107–118). San Francisco, CA: Jossey-Bass.

Malaguzzi, L. (1994). Your image of the child: Where teaching begins. *Exchange, 3*(94). Retrieved from http://www.reggioalliance.org/downloads/malaguzzi:ccie:1994.pdf

National Research Council. (2006). *Learning to think spatially: GIS as a support system in the K–12 curriculum*. Washington, DC: National Academies Press.

Ontario Ministry of Education (2015). Pedagogical documentation: Leading learners in the early years and beyond. Retrieved from http://edu.gov.on.ca/eng/literacynumeracy/inspire/research/CBS_PedagogicalDocument.pdf

Ontario Ministry of Education (2012). Students of mystery: The student work study initiative. *LNS* webcast. Retrieved from https://thelearningexchange.ca/projects/students-of-mystery-the-student-work-study-teacher-initiative/

Ontario Ministry of Education. (2014). Collaborative inquiry in Ontario: What we have learned and where are we now. *Capacity Building Series.* Toronto, ON: Queen's Printer for Ontario.

Ontario Ministry of Education (2013). Student voice: Transforming relationships. Retrieved from http://www.edu.gov.on.ca/eng/literacynumeracy/inspire/research/CBS_StudentVoice.pdf

Ontario Ministry of Education (2011a). Learning in the field: The Student Work Study Teachers Initiative 2009-2010. Retrieved from http://www.edu.gov.on.ca/eng/literacy-numeracy/research/swst.pdf

Ontario Ministry of Education (2011b). Maximizing student mathematical learning in the early years. *Capacity Building Series.* Toronto, ON: Queen's Printer for Ontario.

Ontario Ministry of Education (2010a). Communication in the mathematics classroom. *Capacity Building Series.* Toronto, ON: Queen's Printer for Ontario.

Ontario Ministry of Education. (2010b). *The full-day early learning kindergarten program* (draft version). Toronto, ON: Author.

Ontario Ministry of Education. (2010c). Integrated learning in the classroom. *Capacity Building Series.* Toronto, ON: Queen's Printer for Ontario.

Ontario Ministry of Education. (2005). *The Ontario curriculum, grades 1–8: Mathematics.* Toronto, ON: Author.

Ontario Ministry of Education. (2003). *Early math strategy: The Report of the Expert Panel on Early Math in Ontario.* Toronto, ON: Author.

Orb, A., Eisenhauer, L., & Wynaden, D. (2000). Ethics in qualitative research. *Journal of Nursing Scholarship, 33*(10), 93–96.

Oreck, B. (2004). The artistic and professional development of teachers. *Journal of Teacher Education, 55*(1), 55–69.

Parrish, S. (2010). *Number Talks: Helping children build mental math and computation strategies, grades K–5.* Sausalito, CA: Math Solutions.

Planche, B., (2009). Ten powerful conditions for learning. *Quest Journal.* Toronto, ON: York University.

Riveros, A., Newton, P., & Burgess, D. (2012). A situated account of teacher agency and learning: Critical reflections on professional learning communities. *Canadian Journal of Education, 35*(1), 202–216.

Rooyackers, P. (1998). *101 drama games for children.* Alameda, CA: Hunter House.

The Royal Conservatory. (n.d.). LTTA research: Selected findings for LTTA students. Retrieved from https://www.rcmusic.com/learning/ltta/ltta-research

Schein, E. H. (2010). *Organizational culture and leadership* (4th ed., pp. 315–328). San Francisco, CA: Jossey-Bass.

Schnellert, L., & Butler, D. L. (2016). Teachers as self- and co-regulating learners: We should reconceptualise teacher development as collaborative inquiry [Web log post]. *Psychology Today.* APA Division 15.Retrieved from https://www.psychologytoday.com/blog/psyched/201612/teachers-self-and-co-regulating-learners

Schnellert, L., & Butler, D. L. (2014). Collaborative inquiry: Empowering teachers in their professional development. *Education Canada, 54*(3), 18–22. Retrieved from https://www.edcan.ca/articles/collaborative-inquiry/

Shreeves, R. (1990). *Children dancing* (2nd ed.). New York, NY: Ward Lock Educational.

Smylie, M., & Hart, A. (2000). School leadership for teacher learning and change: A human and social capital development perspective. In J. Murphy & K. S. Louis

(Eds.), *Handbook of research on educational administration* (2nd ed.). San Francisco, CA: Jossey-Bass.

Stepanek, J., Appel, G., Leong, M., Turner Mangan, M., & Mitchell, M. (2007). *Leading lesson study: A practical guide for teachers and facilitators.* Thousand Oaks, CA: Corwin.

Stoll, L. (2009). Capacity building for school improvement or creating capacity for learning? A changing landscape. *Journal of Educational Change, 10*(2–3), 115–127.

Swartz, L. (2002). *The new drama themes* (3rd ed.). Markham, ON: Pembroke.

Tarr, P. (2011). Reflections and shadows: Ethical issues in pedagogical documentation. *Canadian Children, 36*(2), 11–16.

Taylor, W. (2007). Conscious competence learning model. London, UK: BusinessBalls. Retrieved from http://www.businessballs.com/consciouscompetencelearningmodel.htm#fifth-stage-conscious-competence

Timperley, H., & Alton-Lee, A. (2008). Reframing teacher professional learning: An alternative policy approach to strengthening valued outcomes for diverse learners. *Review of Research in Education, 32*(1), 328–369.

van Veen, K., Zwart, R. & Meirink, J. (2012). What makes teacher professional learning effective? A literature review. In M. Kooy & K. van Veen (eds.) *Teacher learning that matters: An International Perspective.* New York, NY: Routledge.

West, L. (2012). Leaders in educational thought [Video]. Retrieved from http://www.curriculum.org/secretariat/leaders/lucy.html

Wien, C. A. (2008). *Emergent curriculum in the primary classroom: Interpreting the Reggio Emilia approach in schools.* New York, NY: Teachers College Press.

Wien, C. (2004). From policing to participation: Overturning the rules and creating amiable classrooms. *Young Children, 59*(1), 34–40.

York-Barr, J., & Duke, K. (2004). What do we know about teacher leadership? Findings from two decades of scholarship. *Review of Educational Research, 74*(3), 255–316.

Index